From Christian To χριστιανός (Christian)

ISBN 978-1-7321613-0-6

GRACE   LOVE   FAITH   TRUTH   KINGDOM

© 2023 Marvin L. Andrus Sr.

ALL RIGHTS RESERVED. REPRODUCTION IN WHOLE OR IN PART WITHOUT WRITTEN PERMISSION IS PROHIBITED.

Printed in USA:

I BEAR STRONG AND VISIBLE WITNESS OF THE PALM RETENTIVE ATTENTION AND AFFECTION OF MY GOD. KEEP GOD FIRST IN YOUR LIFE AND LET HIM AND HIS WORD COVER YOUR 12 AND 6, FROM THE GRACE OF GOD AND MY LOVE TO YOU!!!

Scriptures are from King James and New International version of the bible.

Self-Published

GRACE LOVE FAITH TRUTH KINGDOM

From **Christian** *To*

χριστιανός

GREEK MEANING CHRISTIAN

*The Revealing of a Living
Lie That Came True*

by

Pastor Marvin L. Andrus Sr.

Table of Contents

Foreword 6
Dedication & Acknowledgments 7
The Author's Wife 8
Endorsements 9
Preface 13
Chapter 1: Life As A Question 14
Chapter 2: Vain Exposure / Truth Reveal 26
Chapter 3: In The Spot Light 39
Chapter 4: Guidance and Choice 48
Chapter 5: Arrival 63
Chapter 6: How We Get There 75
Chapter 7: Released from the Leash 87
Chapter 8: The Military Adult Christian 99
Chapter 9: Time Brings About a Change 115
Chapter 10: Adulterer's Brushes with Death ...127
Chapter 11: Recklessness or Malfeasance 139
Chapter 12: The Repetition of a Husband 148
Chapter 13: Behavior With a Digging Shovel ...156
Chapter 14: The Picture Gets Clearer 169

Chapter 15: A Father with Hope 181

Chapter 16: A Battle of The Causes 194

Chapter 17: Aimlessly Fueling the Flames 205

Chapter 18: If You Desire the Truth 222

Chapter 19: Growth Speaks Vividly 234

Chapter 20: The Slaughtering Type 242

Chapter 21: The Holy Ghost Visits 253

Chapter 22: God's View of Family 263

Chapter 23: The Thanks and Trials 271

Chapter 24: Assignments Can Change 279

Chapter 25: Answers are Necessary 293

Chapter 26: The χριστιανός Lives 301

Chapter 27: Cumulative Thought 308

Appendix: Definitions 316

Foreword

To God be the glory for this life and living. I'm writing the truth to inspire, share, encourage, impact, empower, teach, inform and challenge **YOU**. This book will flow from an ominous beginning through visceral challenges, impulsive decisions and ending at a concrete spiritual position bonded by repentance and deliverance. Its main objective is to get all of us to arrive at this point:

Christ centered, God ordained,

and led by The Holy Spirit.

Dedication & Acknowledgments

Most of all, thanks to my wife, Laura, who inspires and encourages me with her love and support in ministry and life. To my mother Evelyn Andrus, for encouraging me to keep God first in my life. To my son Darius, for your insight and perspective from this dispensation!!! To my relatives, friends, acquaintances and God sent, thanks are in order. For the village of people that babysat, pulled my ears, shared wisdom, displayed positive values and kept me out of harm's way, thank you. For the people who showed me humility and rewarded me for my positive values and work ethic, thank you. Thank you for your continued prayers and well wishes for me and my family. **COME AND ACHIEVE SPIRITUAL MATURITY WITH ME.**

GOD KNOWS YOUR NAME!

The Author's Wife

I have witnessed your transformation and dedication to serve the Lord. You are bold and courageous as a lion and you let the world hear your roar for Christ. That is so awesome!!! You possess the characteristics of a man of God, and God will perfect the things that concern your life. You are a wise, committed, transparent, truthful, honest, righteous, strong and tireless leader and you work hard at maintaining and enhancing your relationship with Jesus Christ. You have a passion to effect change in the community and to unify a coalition of ministry leaders for the greatest impact to be achieved across religious denominations.

I love the strength, tenacity and perseverance that you possess never giving up when it's in God's plan. God ordained this book so that others will be delivered and set free from sin and a vain existence by the guidance and power of The Holy Spirit. I respect, honor and love your candor and insight concerning your past sins and the past vain existence of your life. Marvin, I love you and God has blessed me with a husband that I can truly love and depend on. Thanks for everything that you do!!!

LAURA

Endorsements
Dear Reader

In the pages that lie ahead, you will embark on a remarkable journey. From the moment you start reading, you will be captivated by the love, sacrifice, and unwavering commitment to show the love of God as Marvin pours out what the Lord has led and guided him to bless you with.

Marvin at 58 years of age has been on a journey with the Lord that has seen him through the blessings and challenges of being a Fatherless Teenager, Husband, Father of 3 Sons, Army 1991 Gulf War Combat Veteran, Corrections Officer, Graduate of United Theological Seminary and Bible College (Bachelor Degree), and Pastor (His Light Kingdom Church) in Opelousas, LA.

Worldwide travel and years of sensitive encounters have matured him in ways that have strengthened and equipped him with experiences, wisdom, and knowledge that we as people can glean from for the betterment of our spirits, our approaches to life, and the Lord.

By the grace of God, the love of Jesus Christ, the guidance of the Holy Ghost, preaching since 2003, and now as a Pastor, Kingdom Builder, and Community Leader, he writes to inspire, enlighten, and move us. You will learn the true essence of what it means to be selfless, to serve others, and to shine a light in the darkest of moments. From evil, ugly, and careless to faithful, resilient, dedicated, and compassionate, you will be inspired, encouraged, and challenged to be a testament to the power that we possess to have a profound impact on the lives of many.

Marvin's impact is far-reaching and transformative. He leads with compassion, kindness, and empathy. His life continuously touches lives, offers guidance, solace, spiritual renewal, and love. By trials and errors, faults and experiences, failures and disappoints, God has taken over and He has complete control as seen in Marvin's faithfulness to Kingdom building and service to the community. The testament as such will be discovered as you are captivated by the wealth of wisdom and knowledge that He has shared with all of us in this profound move of God. Well done Marvin!!!

Dr. Henry H. Cannon
Biblical Precepts, Concepts, and Truths
Seattle, WA

This manuscript is an answer to prayer! Allow me to take you on a personal travel in time to one weekday in December 1998 as I was walking on the Alameda Beach in California, crying my heart out because I had been toyed with for the last time by a man with ill intentions. God's response to me was that He would one day restore a flock of men to the body of Christ. At that time I was unaware that there was a scripture that says this very thing. A few months later while on a personal bible study, I encountered Ezekiel 36 the last two verses, I saw God's promise for a flock of men that would understand loyalty and obedient service:

Ezekiel 36:37-38 AMPC

[37] Thus says the Lord God: For this also I will let the house of Israel inquire of Me to do it for them; *I will increase their men like a flock*. **[38] ... so shall the waste cities be filled with flocks of men; and they shall know, understand, and realize that I am the Lord [the Sovereign Ruler, Who calls forth loyalty and obedient service].**

I didn't meet Marvin until 8 years ago when I was introduced by my husband (Don Turner, one of Marvin's fellow seminarians), who now leads the PORTION of our of Double Portion Kingdom Ministries titled Flock of Men.

In this manuscript Marvin has successfully captured and exposed the heart of religious **CHRISTIAN LIVING LIE** as opposed to someone who is seriously seeking to serve God. One thing that he has done that I had not experienced much of in many church arenas is he has been painfully transparent and honest about his trials and the damage that he has done in the process of recognizing the **CHRISTIAN LIVING LIE**. He has faced himself, he has faced the women in his past, he has faced his children, and he faced God. Any man reading this book will be challenged to do the same or follow the same outline for himself and allow God to be the change agent, changing him from a **CHRISTIAN LIVING LIE** to Christian, a real one, a χριστιανός as he will explain to us. Women will be enlightened and receive insight as to what some of the men in their life may have had to face, or need to confront in their healing process. All people groups, men and women, will be encouraged by reading this book.

Thank you Marvin Andrus of His Light Kingdom Church, and Pastor Laura for this divine kingdom connection! We love both of you dearly! From Dr Paulette Denise Turner and her husband Don K. Turner.

Dr. Paulette Denise Turner
Double Portion Kingdom Ministries
Houston, TX

Preface

HEY Y'ALL, JUST TO LET Y'ALL KNOW, THE QUOTED, CORRESPONDING SCRIPTURES DEALING WITH the word's of Christ that are in red in the bible are in this different font in the text of the book. _PLEASE OVERLOOK THE RUN ON SENTENCES, SPARATIC PUNCTUATION ERRORS, AND THE PROPHANITY USED IN THE AUTHENTIC AND ORIGINAL EXPERIENCES._ **IT REVEALS THE TRUTH IN THE CONFESSIONS AND LIFE. IN THIS MOVE OF GOD THE PLAN IS TO SEE IN WHAT WAS UNTO WHAT IS!!! ACHIEVE SPIRITUAL MATURITY WITH ME.** HUMBLED AND REPENTANT WITH LOVE IN MY HEART AND SPIRIT!!!

Chapter 1: Life As A Question

? ? ?

? LIFE AS A QUESTION ?

? ? ?

What is the answer to the question in life? Conceivable thoughts don't begin to answer the question until we bear the burdens and the experiences in the question itself. The answer is in a Move of God that we as faithful believers must seek after with honor, praise, and glory for the spiritual and authentic answer. My prayer is that we would be righteous by our moral compass for it's where our flesh reigns. We must pull back layer after layer of our questionable existence to answer the question about ourselves. Yes, often we must live through it to receive the answer of it, it being life. In retrospect, life as a question makes since to me because **I lived so much of it in the darkness of humanity's choices**. Living bi-focally, meaning carnally and spiritually, has educated and enlightened me to a capacity that's worthy of my offer unto you.

The eb and flow or wax and wane in life whether pinpoint, peripheral, or hindsight calls for us to tone and perfect mitigative options in our quest to live the question in life. Life, while complex for a plethora of reasons, is not chosen but granted. Life by God's grace that is justified in Jesus by our faith is puzzling for a tyro or novice Christian, but is quite awesome to the true believer! Within the measurements of chosen but granted, lies a key component in life for which praise, worship, and glory are the hallmark for advancement, progression, and success at the Kingdom level in the Name of our Lord and Savior, Jesus Christ!!!

God being The Creator, vital, and key component is necessarily there or present in life when we understand alpha, beginning. In life, we are aimed at damning and destructive behavior in the onset of God's will and purpose for His breath of life. The question in life may be obscured or ambiguous but we must live in the name of Jesus to end and answer the question. God shall remain mysterious and present.

Apply the normal and societal standards to this life and live your greatest holy life, as some would say, but without God the Father, God the Son, and God the Holy Ghost, life is lived meaningless and bleak. Self-treachery or life-treachery from any viewpoint is the birth of humanity so the nature of humankind is to exist in the bondage and sickness of sin.

Job 14:1
Man that is born of a woman is of few days, and full of trouble.

Treachery defined here as the act or an instance of willful betrayal.

Life's questionable existence is justified thru our Lord and Savior Jesus Christ, but He must remain as such. His love, deity, nature, presence, and essence contain the stabilizing approaches to our living which can prevent cataclysmic destruction as we navigate through the quarters, halves, and stages of life.

Justified living gets us to a place that gives God something to work with. Knowing and understanding that justification is a part of the trilogy and tenses of salvation is a landmark and the beginning of a quest for our true east or our spiritual direction. This basic level of justification which is covered by the blood of Jesus Christ, that was shed on His Calvary Cross, moves us to a position in life where our portions of wisdom and knowledge began to multiply causing the question of life to be remitted, remanded, and rebuked. In other words, life shouldn't be a question, but it should be the Will and Purpose of God.

This time in life can be scary and vulnerable, because the forces of evil and wickedness play their role in causing life's question. If you thought who, what, when, where, why, and how were difficult to answer, then you haven't really come to know the magnitude and capability of evil!!! With the murky, disastrous waves of people, circumstances, and situations, lost and confused in life is normal, but prayer, fasting, and supplication are very available to us for spiritual food and spiritual combat. Holy!!!

Maybe we don't want answers. Maybe we just want to remain clueless or oblivious to the true meaning or cause, (GOD), for humankind. Maybe we've just decided to remain on a path that leads to nowhere productive in spirit or truth. Maybe our moral compass has never pointed to the East or

Heaven. If thus is the case, then there is no need for affirmation. I can assure you that in due season the question in life will hinder, maim, cripple, and torment or it will make a monster out of us. I didn't want to be a monster, but when you drag folk along in your darksome, aimless, devotion-less, and unworthy existence so shall a monster we'll be!!!

Get the question in life answered sooner rather than later. It doesn't have to take 39 years to submit. It doesn't have to be answered to the detriment of several innocent people. It doesn't have to smother our children and victimize the ones we love and them that love us. Develop a Christian character that feeds off of the wisdom and the light of the Lord.

GOD KNOWS YOUR NAME!

Please bear with me as I navigate from the *then and there arriving at the here and now*. I pray that as my question in life is placed on full display that repentance, love, and salvation will become your life's spiritual motives and desires. You'll see the word Christian and the word χριστιανός. Christian means **past**. χριστιανός *means **present.*** If a point or thought is misunderstood or unclear, I have created a glossary with definitions in the rear of the book. I became a Minister, but _becoming a child of GOD was salvation for me!!!_ I'll begin with defining **vain** the beginning and approaching point in this span of time in my life. ACHIEVE SPIRITUAL MATURITY WITH ME.

VAIN: without effect or avail; to no purpose. In an improper or irrelevant manner. Ineffectual or unsuccessful; futile. Without real significance, value, or importance; baseless or worthless.

This introduction describes my 39-year span of life before the awakening and quickening of the Holy Spirit. The vain existence isn't acknowledged by many of us, but it's common and real. "From the definition, you can visualize the aimless and fruitless actions of my being." In addition to the aimless and fruitless, Marvin, was the toxic and fracturing person, that you and others were complicit in actions and in relationships void of a sound foundation.

A portrait of me: no intent, no goal, no thought. Awaking on a daily basis functioning as is. Manners, politeness, _churchee_, and southern hospitality were a common place within me because I was born in the south and raised in corporal punishment. I didn't care about Kingdom issues nor did I have any interest in the presence and promises of God.

Some of you will have difficulty or struggle with reading this, because its existence is outside of predictable or reasonable inferences. This **CHRISTIAN LIVING LIE** was not guided by spiritual or normal principles. It existed outside of any gender, racial, ethnic, religious, economic, norms or parameters. For that reason, I must insist that you see, grasp and understand the position and nature of the blessing absent of comprehension. First, absorb the awful behavior, dark and desolate direction traveled, and the vain existence that was succumbed to. If you invest your intellect or formal training on trying to understand the mindset or reasoning in the material of my **CHRISTIAN LIVING LIE**, then you will have made a negligent investment.

GOD KNOWS YOUR NAME!

My **CHRISTIAN LIVING LIE** presents itself to all of you for the lessons, dysfunctions, patterns, issues, problems, disgraces, insights, dilemmas, dramas and torments from a vain existence. It was necessary to quote scripture as I did to aid and assist the tyro Christian and the novice Christian. *This is not the bible rewritten and passed off as a literary masterpiece of the most intellectual or spiritual kind!!!* With a fervent and effectual prayer, I hope that you would understand how important it is to live a Holy Spirit Dwelling and Fruit Filled life. Other people's experiences in life demonstrates and gives us **the what not to do**, if we have the desire to live by what is good and lovely. **Foundational issue!!!**

Galatians 5:22 - 23, 25,26

[22] But the fruit of the Spirit is love, joy, peace, longsuffering, gentleness, goodness, faith, [23] Meekness, temperance: against such there is no law. [25] If we live in the Spirit, let us also walk in the Spirit. [26] Let us not be desirous of vain glory, provoking one another, envying one another.

This fabric of my being was unintentionally devastating to the esteem and desires of those that had a direction they desired to go in life. I own it all from hello to the depths of its abysmal existence and we as χριστιανός and as a society need to own ours as well. Don't make the mistake of focusing on the sex narrative. *The disparaging issues are the lack and negligence of prayer and commitment to* _worship and serve God._ ACHIEVE SPIRITUAL MATURITY WITH ME.

Isaiah 53:4-6

⁴ Surely he hath borne our griefs, and carried our sorrows: yet we did esteem him stricken, smitten of God, and afflicted. ⁵ But he was wounded for our transgressions, he was bruised for our iniquities: the chastisement of our peace was upon him; and with his stripes we are healed. ⁶ All we like sheep have gone astray; we have turned every one to his own way; and the Lord hath laid on him the iniquity of us all.

From the Old Testament scripture above, we are introduced to Our Lord and Savior, Jesus Christ. I thought it necessary to begin the message here, due to the attack that Christianity is under and also how the scripture brings hope and relief to those of us that are burdened with past and present transgressions and iniquities. I'm familiar with the subject, because I attacked the church by my disrespect of the assembly. My acquaintances and relationships didn't fall under the instructions for the χριστιανός and God's assembly, however; my neglect didn't rise to the level of the literary attacks such as; 13 Reasons why I am no longer a Christian, the multi-lateral bible variances, church shootings and others. I have the hope and faith that the church can grow daily and stand up from its dormant and lethargic state.

GOD KNOWS YOUR NAME!

Hebrews 10:22-26

[22] Let us draw near with a true heart in full assurance of faith, having our hearts sprinkled from an evil conscience, and our bodies washed with pure water. [23] Let us hold fast the profession of our faith without wavering; (for he is faithful that promised;) [24] And let us consider one another to provoke unto love and to good works: [25] Not forsaking the assembling of ourselves together, as the manner of some is; but exhorting one another: and so much the more, as ye see the day approaching. [26] For if we sin wilfully after that we have received the knowledge of the truth, there remaineth no more sacrifice for sins,

My view of the church as it exists is similar to that of Dr. Kurt Clark in his book entitled Invisible Institution and Empire. Thou seemingly invisible it is continuously by nature and design fighting the establishment of carnal freedoms and he focused on The Black Church and its invisible struggle to combat the subcommunity beginnings and treatment as such to this day. I fear that the church is in its lethargic and dormant state due in part to age, history and status quo while inherently failing to assist us in prevailing over our transgressions and iniquities.

The framework of the book is all inclusive so my faults as a person, son, father, husband, and Christian are all in the narrative. All of the above were in the structure of my life, and my life was hampered and scarred by my vain existence. Really engross yourself in this menagerie of a life and carnage of time. There's going to be more about the carnage and menagerie later, but more pressing is my failure to follow God's instructions.

The spectrum of my vain actions didn't discriminate against Island women, Asian women, European women, American women or any race, ethnicity or background and it functioned within unlimited boundaries, so from ocean to ocean, continent to continent, and state to state was my parlor of comfort. I didn't have any insatiable issues or desires, so don't try to add a psychological foundation to understand what was occurring. Trust when I say my existence was vain to say the least.

In most of my travels and relationships, folks found me ingratiating and appetizing. Truthfully, I was fractured and fragmented emotionally and spiritually, but above all else, I lacked hope in the resurrection, Holy Ghost's guidance, and affirmative choice. The life experiences in word for word, messy, stinky, provocative, lustful, and impactful detail sets the foundation for us to see the carnal and spiritual flaws; not to mention the invisible hope in the resurrection.

Chapter 2: Vain Exposure / Truth Reveal

Ingratiating and appetizing is what I want to be to you on a spiritual and kingdom level in my pouring out. I'll plead, and beg you to dredge deep into my vain existence while focusing on how I nonchalantly pilfered, and carnaged time without consideration of the future and accusation. My prayer is for us to possess a greater purpose and spiritual goal. BAANG, BAAMB, BOOOM *it's your choice*, but to God be the glory for the things that He has done.

People have abandoned the truth for millenniums. The focus is on Christians, because faith and truth are the foundation and staple of the process for the culmination of our purpose in God. The truth should be our hallmark or signature card that affords us avenues to a prosperous and jovial existence in the Kingdom of God. Once we've abandoned the truth, life takes a vain, vile, vexatious and vicious direction that ultimately leads to regret.

First, we must ask the question, why are we abandoning the truth with such ease and regularity? I understand that the truth cuts like a double-edged sword, but what's the alternative for straying away from it? The answer should be derived from our thoughts and meditations on an eternal stage.

Hebrews 4:12
For the word of God is quick, and powerful, and sharper than any two-edged sword, piercing even to the dividing asunder of soul and spirit, and of the joints and marrow, and is a discerner of the thoughts and intents of the heart.

Looking back over the years, the truth has been extremely difficult to arrive at due to the carnal discomfort and exposure contained within it. If we truly understood the stabbing and slashing that we're imposing on our spirits and living, we would know the awesomeness of truth. The scapegoat tells the truth now for this reason:

John 14:5-7
[5] Thomas saith unto him, Lord, we know not whither thou goest; and how can we know the way? [6] Jesus saith unto him, I am the way, the truth, and the life: no man cometh unto the Father, but by me. [7] If ye had known me, ye

should have known my Father also: and from henceforth ye know him, and have seen him.

Abandoning the truth is done without an inkling or mention of cause and effect. With truth, we can save ourselves from the damaging after effects from the revelation of its origin. Every situation or circumstance began its existence in truth before the truth was abandoned. A major question should be infused in our spirits. What is best for me, the truth or the lie? We can equate that to the phrase greater, greatest good. Cause and affect contain the answer. In considering truth, place specific attention and focus on destination. Where are you trying to arrive and what are you trying to achieve? The stand for truth creates an insatiable desire in faith for God's Word.

Before we go deeper into truth and what it looks like, please let me share some truth with you. The brother that I was closest to was older than me. I was fourteen-years-old and he wanted to take me to stay with him in Tulsa, Oklahoma for a few weeks. He came in drunk at 3am after having sex, and committing adultery, with one of his old flames from way back. She was married as well, but don't ask me where her husband was or what lie she told him to be out having sex with my brother until three in the morning. He had several of such affairs in different states and towns.

He tossed me the keys and said, "you're driving." He gave me a couple of instructions and told me when to wake him up. While staying with him in Tulsa, we got high every day. Smoking weed and drinking gin with his fourteen-year-old brother didn't seem to bother him. He kept marijuana sitting on the living room table like it was candy. He verbally and physically fought with his wife while I was there and in my presence.

About twenty years later in a conversation with him, I asked him are you still messing with that dope? No was his reply. On a visit to Tulsa with my mother on the way to California a few years later, he asked me to borrow money to get a few items and some food for the house. He spent very little time with me and our mother. A little later, he asked me if I could get him some gas until his check came in. We got in the car and made a stop before we went to the gas station. After returning home from the gas station, he still paid very little attention to me and our mother.

I went to the bedroom where I found him doing a hit of crack cocaine. I was devastated and hurt, so much so, that it brought me to tears. Mom wanted to know what was wrong, but the only thing that I could tell her was that we were leaving in the morning. I slept for a few hours and we departed. He nor I said goodbye and he didn't tell our mother bye nor did she ever ask why we departed in the manner that we did. The one brother that I had some semblance of a relationship with was a crack addict.

How long does it take?

GOD KNOWS YOUR NAME!

Over the years, I had sent and loaned him thousands of dollars trying to help him and his family maintain or maybe get ahead. This was the revelation to a χριστιανός that bites and stings when it comes, but χριστιανόςs should constantly pray for the revelations of life. He and I hadn't spoken for some time and one day he decided to call me to tell me that he was contemplating suicide. I shrugged him off when he told me that he wanted to kill himself. It never dawned on me to think of the negative issues that he was going through at the time.

Growing up not knowing who his father was and not being a father to his two older daughters, and struggling with his drug addiction, and the possibility of two children from an adulterous affair of which was part of the reason why his wife alienated herself from him was visible. The Lord knows the worst of it. In life and living most of the time when love and respect is trampled on or damaged, they are unrecoverable.

The husband with four children that we know of, the brother who was the life of the gathering, the brother that was clearly my mother's favorite is set to kill himself. We talked for three hours that day and we laughed and joked. I hung up with the sense that everything was okay. A week later, I received a phone call from my mother and she said that my brother had killed himself by hanging himself at the facility that he was going to for rehab and treatment. She really had a few miserable years with guilt because she thought that if she would've known about the addiction when we left his home years ago, that she would've stopped him from being an addict. You and I know the truth in that thought.

That outcome was visceral, but I chose to act from assumption and neutrality. I started to ask myself some questions. Did he kill himself for the insurance money to pay me back? Did he do this to relieve the grief that he obviously was feeling from disappointing me? Did he kill himself for the money to feed his family and stop the hurt he was causing? *How long does it take?* Does it get any heavier than that? Yes it does!!! Sometimes we can't see GOD in all that we do, but life would be so enlightening if we did things in the name of Holy Spirit, Jesus and GOD! The truth had come calling on our family and with it remained the question *how long does it take.*

Another book could be written about truth in and of itself. For a χριστιανός, there's no other option greater than acknowledging the truth and its omniscient correlation. It's important and imperative that we know the reward affiliated with truth and the decimation of vain existence. Our works as χριστιανόςs should be done in truth and unending worship which is tried by the fire.

1 Corinthians 3:13-15

[13] Every man's work shall be made manifest: for the day shall declare it, because it shall be revealed by fire; and the fire shall try every man's work of what sort it is. [14] If any man's work abide which he hath built thereupon, he shall receive a reward. [15] If any man's work shall be

burned, he shall suffer loss: but he himself shall be saved; yet so as by fire.

At the onset, the truth is found in God and the heart of humankind. With this knowledge, we can live in spirit and in truth, free from vain ideations and our vain lies. From Christian to χριστιανός is being written for that reason. I pray and hope that 39 years of a **CHRISTIAN LIVING LIE** doesn't occur in your life and the *prevention* of the nature in lying is accepted, consecrated, and ordained. Read and understand this now because my foundation to becoming and adult or χριστιανός doesn't have to be the blueprint for the future.

There isn't one day that I have awakened and intentionally had evil, malice or reckless intent in my heart or purpose. I was taught and raised by my mother to love people from all walks of life, to be responsible for my actions, and to keep God first in my life. My behavior in success or demise wasn't callous in any fashion. I didn't have a morbid desire to be ingratiating to anyone in particular. I didn't have an insatiable problem with any actions that we involve ourselves in outside of the Word of God.

Intellect and reason won't help you learn from my **CHRISTIAN LIVING LIE**.

My functioning, while aimless and fruitless attracted goal oriented and focused folks that knew I was married and they touched my wedding ban, but they desired me in a marital concept. After years of sharing these types of stories, my faults, experiences, travels, accomplishments, encounters, and relationship issues with my wife, Laura, and those close to me, the time has come for me to help or prevent others from the unnecessary carnage of time in a life. This has been a painstaking journey that can be avoided, if we choose <u>*"spirit over intellect and faith over senses."*</u>

What you are about to read is decades of faulty actions, faulty commitments, faulty principles, faulty religion, faulty decisions, and faulty relationships that made up my existence, but it won't stop there. More importantly and imperatively, you'll receive the positive aspects of my living, and the deliverance obtained from those faulty decades. I'm currently living delivered in this decade and for decades to come, and I'm blessed to see the fruition of this journey. The amount or peak of distress and faults in your journey depends on whether or not you decide to pursue life by the grace of God and the life experiences of those before and around you.

I caught an episode of *Iyanla Fix My Life* and she was assisting and counseling a few gentlemen that had been recently released from prison. She was focusing on getting them to understand why society wouldn't accept them back into the community or be willing to grant them a chance to be inclusive. Iyanla advised them to free their minds and spirits from all the rough times until now.

Then she told them that they had to own the situations and circumstances that had gotten them to a prison sentence. The premise behind owning their plight would open avenues to assist them in understanding the legitimate concerns people harbor for the previously incarcerated. Today, I am free in mind and spirit from the prison of vain actions and I take ownership of my faults, disregards, babblings, destructive actions, mental complacencies, and disasters.

GOD KNOWS YOUR NAME!

Most books written from the Christian or Spiritual point of view, often tells us about how sin, sins, and sinning unravel us, and how it leads to our demise or bitter end. They're scripture laced with no actual personal reference or party to the topic, iniquity, transgression or calamity, and if they did commit such acts, they don't want us to know, but not so with this unorthodox, literary adventure. I believe that if the books were actually written by χριστιανός and not Christians, that we would find enlightenment and wisdom versus sin being the end and the prosperity route to salvation.

Every word, phrase and quote used in this book is written for true accuracy and maximum effect on a common and sensible level including the distinction of religion, socio-economic, gender, race, ethnicity, and conversation etc.! This is just me, a simple man and a common man not profoundly or prophetically writing, and writing without any particular style or format. The events and times crossover each other intermittently, but the book flows smoothly. The delivery method is not as important as the message delivered in truth and content. My sins, iniquities, calamities, and unrighteousness will be reverberated a few times to keep you informed and on the same page with me.

I must plead with you that as you read, engross, and invoke yourself into this tool and precursor for life, that you receive it as a move of

God to head off, cut off, and drop off any and all of the entanglements of our adversary, Satan. The world is his play ground, and we, by birth, in the wisdom and knowledge of the first man Adam will arbitrarily and un-arbitrarily act and be guided by his playbook. Heaven and Hell are real eternal **choices**. They are both a prepared place for prepared people.

With most of the study and reading that I've done, Hell seems to be a place and topic that authors are steering away from. To deliver an authentic message, it must contain the spiritual variables, inferences, suggestions, and outcomes both implicit and explicit in the realm of God's will and purpose. Without such candor and frankness, the Majesty, Dominion, Supremacy, and Grace of God is watered down and hidden in jargon. ACHIEVE SPIRITUAL MATURITY!!!

By now, I know that you've seen **GOD KNOWS YOUR NAME!** inserted and spiritually placed in a few places. God knows your name is the answer to how long does it take and it's also the soothing knowledge for our pain and weariness!!! I was introduced to the fact of it by the worldly less fortunate, but the spirit of joy filled performers for God. God knowing our name is a game changer. The spectrum of the sentence is such of a magnitude that it is too kind and too blunt for any reasonable or intellectual measurement. The world hasn't any scale to measure the weight that it lifts or carries. God knows your name is the searing of our heart and the source of our spirit. Marvel at its presence and glory as it appears!

PLEASE!!!
DON'T GET CAUGHT UP OR ENAMORED WITH THE MESSY, EXPLICIT FACTS AND DETAILS, THEY EXIST TO LEARN FROM AND TO TEACH!!!

Chapter 3: In The Spot Light

For the information contained within my writing, I must apologize to the people that find discomfort or exposure in what is revealed. The discomfort comes from reading the details, and knowing that you've lived a Christian lie as well. Or you might read the verbiage and wonder how a χριστιανός could use such language.

Exposure is in the same category. The Lord sheds light on all things for a χριστιανός and I'm glad that His light shines bright in me. If you or what you've been is exposed, then I apologize from the point of understanding that you didn't want the truth or the light to shed on you just yet. I've had to take some harsh criticism about my past, because it has tarnished some of the unknown about my life.

I can speak of these issues because I possessed the chameleon rhetoric, emotion, and existence that wanted so desperately to live on unexposed. I apologize to my family, acquaintances, and friends for the hurt or frustration that my writing may cause. This is not an attempt to shame, disgrace, or befuddle any of you. I just want to be clear and concise without marginalizing the information or the truth.

GOD KNOWS YOUR NAME!

<u>*My living is for the Lord and I am not any of the following:*</u> thief, whoremonger, aimless, down low, drug addict, sex addict, adrenalin junkie, player, impulsive, adulterer, liar, babbler, cheater, evil, abusive, reckless, fornicator, alcoholic, philanderer, careless, murderer, vain, homosexual, gay or heartbroken nor do I possess any phobias. Realize that all sin or sins are not listed. Truth being told is the omittance of sin and darkness, because that's where humanity judges us. Let's not be naive or hypocritical.

I have descended from my bastard's way of living and confess the Lord Jesus by recognizing the shedding of His blood for the remission of my sin. Sin is ongoing and sins have already transpired. Due to our prayer and faith in God, we know that we've won the race and battle and that we're superior to evil.

Hebrews 12:7-9

⁷ If ye endure chastening, God dealeth with you as with sons; for what son is he whom the father chasteneth not? ⁸ But if ye be without chastisement, whereof all are partakers, then are ye bastards, and not sons. ⁹ Furthermore we have had fathers of our flesh which corrected us, and we gave them reverence: shall we not much rather be in subjection unto the Father of spirits, and live?

GOD KNOWS YOUR NAME!

My life was saturated with good and evil, but it leaned more toward a vain existence. For the majority of my adolescent years, I used 23 hours of everyday fueled by impulsive decisions. 23 hours a day is the length of time that the super, awful incarcerated, inmates spend locked behind closed doors in their tiny jail cells. AND I WAS TRUTHLESSLY AND VAINLY LOCKED UP!!! This book should be held in esteem as a life changing situational "do's and do not's" precursor for the adventures in life and your service to the Lord. More important to know is the fact that we can be made whole again.

Acts 4:8-10

8 Then Peter, filled with the Holy Ghost, said unto them, Ye rulers of the people, and elders of Israel, **9** If we this day be examined of the good deed done to the impotent man, by what means he is made whole; **10** Be it known unto you all, and to all the people of Israel, that by the name of Jesus Christ of Nazareth, whom ye crucified, whom God raised from the dead, even by him doth this man stand here before you whole.

When we have gone as far as we can go in the wrong direction, we shouldn't be discouraged because God determines what the last mile in our way will be. I had a transgression and iniquity encyclopedia of a life until I arrived at this point: **READ PSALM 51!!!**

GOD KNOWS YOUR NAME!

Psalm 51

1 Have mercy upon me, O God, according to thy lovingkindness: according unto the multitude of thy tender mercies blot out my transgressions. **2** Wash me throughly from mine iniquity, and cleanse me from my sin. **3** For I acknowledge my transgressions: and my sin is ever before me. **4** Against thee, thee only, have I sinned, and done this evil in thy sight: that thou mightest be justified when thou speakest, and be clear when thou judgest. ⁵ Behold, I was shapen in iniquity; and in sin did my mother conceive me. ⁶ Behold, thou desirest truth in the inward parts: and in the hidden part thou shalt make me to know wisdom. ⁷ Purge me with hyssop, and I shall be clean: wash me, and I shall be whiter than snow. ⁸ Make me to hear joy and gladness; that the bones which thou hast broken may rejoice. ⁹ Hide thy face from my sins, and blot out all mine iniquities. ¹⁰ Create in me a clean heart, O God; and renew a right spirit within me. ¹¹ Cast me not away from thy presence; and take not thy holy spirit from me. ¹² Restore unto me the joy of thy salvation; and uphold me with thy free spirit. ¹³ Then will I teach transgressors thy ways; and sinners shall be converted unto thee. ¹⁴ Deliver me from bloodguiltiness, O God, thou God of my salvation: and my tongue shall sing aloud of thy righteousness. ¹⁵ O Lord, open thou my lips; and my mouth shall shew forth thy praise. ¹⁶ For thou desirest not sacrifice; else would I give it: thou delightest not in burnt offering. ¹⁷ The sacrifices of God are a broken spirit: a broken and a contrite heart, O God, thou wilt not despise. ¹⁸ Do good in thy good pleasure unto Zion: build thou the walls of Jerusalem. ¹⁹ Then shalt thou be pleased with the sacrifices of righteousness, with burnt offering and whole burnt offering: then shall they offer bullocks upon thine altar.

GOD KNOWS YOUR NAME!

<u>If David could pray for forgiveness and promise to serve, we can!!!</u>

This is important to know, I did an abundance of great things and accomplished a great deal during the time that I'm writing about. My family was a people that would give you the shirt off their back if you needed it. I helped a great deal of people and supported others in their efforts to do positive things for themselves and others. For the majority of my adolescent years, I financially supported my family, friends, and acquaintances whenever I could if they needed it. My heart has always been filled with charity and love, but my vain existence precluded me from displaying the effectual fervor of my heart for God.

Before you want to create a back lash at, or for me, know that it is from the warmth of my heart that I'm willing to go through the discomfort and exposure with and for you. I failed to live for something, so I fell for anything, but the joy is in the now, from the road that I've traveled. My message is promoting the fact that _we can do better if we choose to._ Please search the scripture to ensure viability and contextual understanding. As you search the scripture, pray for The Holy Spirit to search your heart.

GOD KNOWS YOUR NAME!

A χριστιανός or spiritual book can't exist without the presence of God's Word, for what is contained within it, is our destiny.

Romans 1:15-17

[15] So, as much as in me is, I am ready to preach the gospel to you that are at Rome also. [16] For I am not ashamed of the gospel of Christ: for it is the power of God unto salvation to every one that believeth; to the Jew first, and also to the Greek. [17] For therein is the righteousness of God revealed from faith to faith: as it is written, The just shall live by faith.

You'll find some scripture verses contained within, but you'll have to search them for yourself and not just at my word. Be overzealous in searching for the message in complete and full context. Read and search various versions of the bible, because there's meat in all of them. In mature and graphic detail, you'll learn where our indulgences and propensities to sin can drag, or lead us. This was my past adolescent years of living that capitulated to the fruition of God's grace and mercy over my life. There's joy in my living now and His countenance remains in my heart and spirit.

Some of you may find an avenue to persecute, slander, ridicule, or mock me, but you're receiving this as my spirit is led to give it to you. I'm the scapegoat or the example beleaguered and then rejuvenated prepared to put me out there for the faith and hope of others. At the completion of my pouring out, you'll understand why we abandon the truth. It is my prayer that you'll gain the confidence and wisdom from this moment on to come clean stripped bare before the presence of The Holy Spirit, allowing your circumstances, situations, trials, and tribulations to be heard.

Leviticus 16:8-10

⁸ And Aaron shall cast lots upon the two goats; one lot for the Lord, and the other lot for the scapegoat. ⁹ And Aaron shall bring the goat upon which the Lord's lot fell, and offer him for a sin offering. ¹⁰ But the goat, on which the lot fell to be the scapegoat, shall be presented alive before the Lord, to make an atonement with him, and to let him go for a scapegoat into the wilderness.

Chapter 4: Guidance and Choice

I bear strong and visible witness to the clutches of Satan, my use as a Devil and the PALM RETENTIVE ATTENTION and AFFECTION OF MY GOD!!! *I have changed the names of the majority of the people involved in this* **CHRISTIAN LIVING LIE** except for the people that I really need to let them know how truly grateful I am for their contribution to my well-being and the positive influences that they were in areas that I would've surely faltered. This literary teaching and informational opportunity were made manifest by repenting from all unrighteousness and then claiming and forming a new relationship with The Father, GOD. This Christian and Spiritual testimony tells us about the existence of sin, and that sins and sinning isn't the end!!!

The major problem or issue is the absence of guidance and choice. The ransom for sin has been paid, but our propensity to sin is in the spiritual makeup of all humankind. Thereto lays the reason for us, at the encouragement of the Apostle Paul, to be our best Olympic person dedicated to soldiering while striving for love, life and the eternal Heaven. In our lives of searching and reaching for the grace of God and the eternal life that He gives, we must focus on _guidance and choice_. Prayer ushers in thoughts and actions and thoughts and actions should exist to please God.

Critically speaking, it's vital to our soul's salvation to immediately start acknowledging and accepting responsibility for our spiritual and carnal actions. We must descent from our bastard's life by receiving and accepting the chastening of God. The quickening Holy Spirit is waiting for us to arrive at this mature state. It's at this point that guidance and choice begin to co-exist, co-mingle, co-guide and co-protect.

One needs the other and the other won't function properly without our proper praying, fasting, relationship, and mutual acceptance. Make a determination and join the struggle.

1 Peter 5:6-10

⁶ Humble yourselves therefore under the mighty hand of God, that he may exalt you in due time: ⁷ Casting all your care upon him; for he careth for you. ⁸ Be sober, be vigilant; because your adversary the devil, as a roaring lion, walketh about, seeking whom he may devour: ⁹

Whom resist stedfast in the faith, knowing that the same afflictions are accomplished in your brethren that are in the world. ¹⁰ But the God of all grace, who hath called us unto his eternal glory by Christ Jesus, after that ye have suffered a while, make you perfect, stablish, strengthen, settle you.

Compare that day to this day and remember the analyst for the day of your testimony. Make your testimony spiritually true and not conquest oriented. Someone needs to hear, know, and experience our journey, for in it is our victory in Christ, Jesus. It's a difficult challenge to get out, but here it is.

GOD KNOWS YOUR NAME!

While reading this, you might make the assumption that I lied a great deal or spoke several untruths, to the contrary. I spoke clearly, concisely, and truthfully treating everyone with dignity and respect. The lies were told to my wives so I could hide my vain actions from them. I didn't use profane language nor did I call anyone out of their name with such language.

When we are presented with choices, our χριστιανός ethics should play a major role in the process of arriving at our choice. Our choices may also contain a visceral element; largely in part for the wisdom and knowledge we already possess and the urge to proceed without guidance. On a basic level of the issue, we would think one would choose the lesser of two evils. Christians living a lie have the capability to put us in that predicament. A predicament that causes a disruption, or confusion bringing our Christian ethics into question. As a **CHRISTIAN LIVING LIE**, I represented that predicament. If we had to choose a person to have some sort of a relationship, we would probably choose, or determine that the person treating us with dignity and respect is better than the opposite.

GOD KNOWS YOUR NAME!

In my situation my treating others with dignity and respect was part of my Christian character, therefore; my **CHRISTIAN LIVING LIE** was the worst of two evils. In other words, it appeared that the greater greatest good was the choice that was made. Please watch, hear, and pray to make spiritual choices. That's our protection from relationship and life issues that are flawed and deceptive.

I heard the prayers of a young man asking the Lord to assist us in being better Christians. My spirit suddenly went "huh?" Christians focus heavily on trying to paint a picture of serene harmony and perfect bliss while sliding down slippery slopes. The lie of bliss and harmony blockades the true struggles and diverts our prayers that ought to ask the Lord for assistance in being a better child of God versus a better Christian.

Not purposed in the heart or sanctioned by Satan, Christians walk and talk a bastard's life failing to seek the inherent adoption of God, His will, His purpose and His glory. I'm not waring against praying for Christ to be our redemptive blessing, but without God there is no Christ. If we can realize the foundation of being a child of God, then we can see to fruition the harmony and bliss of being a χριστιανός. Chat with The Holy Spirit about it. The adopted child of God manifests, and transcends _"From Christian to χριστιανός."_ **Past to Present.**

At 58 years of age and a graduate of United Theological Seminary and Bible College, Monroe, Louisiana, I'm very secure, cemented and rooted in my χριστιανός walk, so if you're thinking oh, another scripture laced poor example of sub-par creative mal-nourishment, back up and think again!!! You're on the side of the fence that is brutal, uncaring, in capable of love and honest in all wrong doing. It's time to take off the gloves and fight the fight that God wants us to fight without being road blocked by the secrets and the truth of our wrong doings.

The honesty mentioned above keeps most of us hanging on, praying, hoping, pleading, and waiting for the wrong doing to shift into a life of glorious, and peaceful bliss. In order for the fulfillment of that peaceful bliss, spiritual bridges have to be designed and constructed by the grace and the never-ending love of God. I'm so joyful and ecstatic that I serve my God, a God that is so just, warm, forgiving, understanding, ingratiating and inviting. He overlooks my faults and abides in me for the work concerning His plan of salvation.

1 Corinthians 15:9-11

⁹ For I am the least of the apostles, that am not meet to be called an apostle, because I persecuted the church of God. ¹⁰ But by the grace of God I am what I am: and his grace which was bestowed upon me was not in vain; but I laboured more abundantly than they all: yet not I, but

the grace of God which was with me. ¹¹ Therefore whether it were I or they, so we preach, and so ye believed.

1 John 5:11-12
¹¹ And this is the record, that God hath given to us eternal life, and this life is in his Son. ¹² He that hath the Son hath life; and he that hath not the Son of God hath not life.

"*From Christian to χριστιανός*" is not meant to tell all, but it tells all as the word of God leads us to do for our healing from the bondage and sickness of sin. I'm sure that some young man or woman will come to gratifying, life altering knowledge, and find the answers to a great deal of questions once they've had this read. This is a pragmatic view, a common view of drugs, alcohol, stealing, sex, adultery, gambling, suicide, sodomy, and depression directly and indirectly as Satan uses it in our lives and society. This means don't look for the un-dotted I's, and un-crossed T's, or the scriptures quoted from the bible just to fill pages, but try to imagine and put you where I've been; ocean to ocean, state to state, and continent to continent.

NOW REALIZE GOD STEPPING IN.

James 5:13-16

[13] Is any among you afflicted? let him pray. Is any merry? let him sing psalms. [14] Is any sick among you? let him call for the elders of the church; and let them pray over him, anointing him with oil in the name of the Lord: [15] And the prayer of faith shall save the sick, and the Lord shall raise him up; and if he have committed sins, they shall be forgiven him. [16] Confess your faults one to another, and pray one for another, that ye may be healed. The effectual fervent prayer of a righteous man availeth much.

Keep in mind the length of the list of transgressions, iniquities, and calamities, because it's going to come up again later. Also at some point, you'll receive some tidbits about relationships, such as; humble your rhetoric and tone. The bible exists to instruct us in loving God and in loving people. God's love is never-ending meaning that a person, place or thing can't stop, or remove the presence of God's love.

GOD KNOWS YOUR NAME!

When we come to the mature and true knowledge of that fact, then we'll be able to love and trust on a new level. That's how we should take our daily living into the process of relationships. Love is never ending and shouldn't be defeated by, disagreements, catastrophe, death, betrayal, or disrespect. _Love is the reason._ _Love is everything._ _Love is eternal._

After gaining the wherewithal to contemplate and reflect on the spiritual things in life, I came to the conclusion of the fact that I thought only of pleasing my flesh. If this had been an addiction or an insatiable desire, Satan would have won or conquered another soul. My daily existence contained that single propulsion to feed my worldly living by seeing to it that other's worldly living was fed as well. A mere vain existence that profited nothing in the way of God's plan or God's will for my living.

I wasn't living by the spirit, so I accumulated more than my share of sour beginnings and outcomes. If it's our intention on becoming pleasing to God and charitable to His people, we must avail ourselves to prayer, fasting, definition, and repentance. By definition, I mean being able to call it what it is. Clearly, I needed to be made whole again. Whole again, as in knowing I'm justified in Christ and praying for the indwelling Holy Spirit to remain upon my life, because our living shouldn't be in vain.

1 John 1:4-9

[4] And these things write we unto you, that your joy may be full. [5] This then is the message which we have heard of him, and declare unto you, that God is light, and in him is no darkness at all. [6] If we say that we have fellowship with him, and walk in darkness, we lie, and do not the truth: [7] But if we walk in the light, as he is in the light, we have fellowship one with another, and the blood of Jesus Christ his Son cleanseth us from all sin. [8] If we say that we have no sin, we deceive ourselves, and the truth is not in us. [9] If we confess our sins, he is faithful and just to forgive us our sins, and to cleanse us from all unrighteousness.

Mahalia Jackson put it like this:

"If I can help somebody, as I travel along"
"If I can help somebody, with a word or song"
"If I can help somebody, from doing wrong"
"No, my living shall not be in vain"
"No, my living shall not be in vain"

GOD KNOWS YOUR NAME!

By the guidance of the Lord and my choice in spirit and in truth to serve GOD, I can humbly, peacefully, and joyfully live my life as sung by Mahalia Jackson.

1 Corinthians 15:57-58
⁵⁷ But thanks be to God, which giveth us the victory through our Lord Jesus Christ. ⁵⁸ Therefore, my beloved brethren, be ye stedfast, unmoveable, always abounding in the work of the Lord, forasmuch as ye know that your labour is not in vain in the Lord.

I helped many along the way for positive reasons, but a thousand great things are wiped out by one awful deed. That is why we should take this route: *By the grace of God, through the blood of Jesus, with the work of the Holy Spirit.*

From an extremely young age, this journey took several life altering, twist and turns dredged in damaging sinful behavior and acts. Only the blood of Jesus could protect a χριστιανός from what could've been his definitive demise due to the absence of guidance and choice. A difference exists between living in the world and being of the world. To heed the warning before the destruction, just be in and of God with our choices.

GOD KNOWS YOUR NAME!

Proverbs 16:18
Pride goeth before destruction, and an haughty spirit before a fall.

Excuses and denials were being conjured up during this time for use at a later date when the cost of living for nothing and standing for indulgence was to be collected. It's always somebody else's fault is the Christian's moniker. In this particular journey, accountability is singular in focus and judgement. It's best for us to obtain spiritual merits while living a balanced life. Our journeys structured in balance should be consecrated in the unanimity of life and love.

The absence of guidance when we are in the mystery and adolescence of life leads us to immoral and unspeakable acts that we can't speak of occurring as we become teenagers and adults. Now in this dispensation and time, those acts are common place and protected by the law of the land and the voice of the people. Where do we go from here isn't a question anymore because consideration from a spiritual stand point has given way to the politics of humankind.

GOD KNOWS YOUR NAME!

I find it not so easy to remember being a little boy. I do remember stealing as a child and being destructive to other people's property. No, I'm not using my father's early departure from this life to his spiritual rest as the means to an end. I will tell you that he, even though guidance was present and taught, was an absentee daddy. Mom tried with every fiber of her being to teach us how to be men, but when provisions have to be first on the menu of life, then absentee mother is the case as well.

So, who is to blame for the darksome choices that we make as children in the world? Who do we point the finger at for the theft of a child's innocence and purity? Who guides and manipulates our actions as children when daddy and mama are unavailable? Who could have such control over our lives that we can't remove ourselves from such behavior? Who carries such power that resistance in any form is futile? Who moves and operates through us from puberty to hospice needs?

Psalm 51:5

Behold, I was shapen in iniquity; and in sin did my mother conceive me.

If you haven't received it by now, I've been speaking with you about the deepest, darkest parts of my life as candid, tactful, moral, and spiritual as I could. What should you take away from what has been written to this point is that God is ever present and there in our time of need, but CHOICE is His method, way, and desire. From the therapist point of view, "It is what It is." From my point of view, Satan has been part of my up bringing and he has taught me a great deal about making my immoral and detrimental mark in this world! Once he has taught us at an early age, he doesn't have to do a refresher course because we do well as shapened sinners to pass the lessons on to our kindred and acquaintances. The wise man said this:

Romans 7:18-20

[18] For I know that in me (that is, in my flesh,) dwelleth no good thing: for to will is present with me; but how to

perform that which is good I find not. [19] For the good that I would I do not: but the evil which I would not, that I do. [20] Now if I do that I would not, it is no more I that do it, but sin that dwelleth in me.

Far from the Prodigal Son am I, but the season and choice has come and been made to turn some things around in this wretched living of mine.

Chapter 5: Arrival

A Sunday morning thirty-nine years in the making of a χριστιανός was about to start. Just another day that appeared to be the same as any other day, but something happened. I put on my Sunday regalia, my church attire, and moseyed my way down the freeway to St. John Baptist Church, of Tacoma, Washington. There was my membership and church affiliation. The Pastor Lee Arthur Madison was delivering his weekly sermon and folks were praising and saying amen in agreement with the message.

Suddenly in the KERYGMA, the meet of the message, he said, "In the year that King Uzziah died" and he began to speak diligently and masterfully about the young prophet Isaiah and at that moment it was the dawn of a new spirit. Some would say, that the light came on, or I smartened up, or I found a greener grass. No, it wasn't magic in a bottle either. What actually happened was the moment I received my salvation and calling to the gospel ministry in April of 2004, a day that was thirty-nine years in the making. Arrived, consecrated and ordained by The Father, signed by

Jesus Christ and witnessed by The Holy Spirit!!! I'm not equating this period in my life to the prodigal son, but I did walk away from my established means as an adult a few times. Now it's time to expose the **CHRISTIAN LIVING LIE**. As I engulfed my spirit into the joy of the moment, I was reminded of the song "He Touched Me."

Volumes could be written about the touch of God. Masterfully crafted, it is filled with several astonishing and amazing wonders. When He touches, there's a new and remarkable means to an end. With the touch from God, we rebuke flesh and blood and profess spirit and soul. It is imperative that we pray and live under His touch less we fall to a reprobated existence. Solidify your heavenly goal by feeling, seeing and knowing His touch.

There must be a way for me to emphatically enunciate about the living lie that became true. You can live a lifetime and never fully and mentally comprehend or notice the lie or lies that we are living. For instance, just look back at something your parents may have said to you in your impressionable days many years ago that stuck with you until now and analyze it from what you know about life and living today.

Just to give you an example; your mother, in her frustration, tells you, "Once an adulterer, always an adulterer." That is a damning and condemning statement, but with further knowledge and wisdom you would come to know that that proverb is utterly, completely, and totally false.

Luke 6:37

Judge not, and ye shall not be judged: condemn not, and ye shall not be condemned: forgive, and ye shall be forgiven:

In view of that proverb and what I know now, I can discontinue to live a lie. The lie being that, I'll never be forgiven for the divorce of my first marriage that I entered into at the age of twenty-four. I cheated and had several sexual affairs and escapades, to include her best friend at the time. If God removes hope and repentance, then what is there to live for? If a personal relationship with the Father, GOD, isn't established or is non-existent then humanity shall have its way. God's word, the Bible, will be of no use to us absent of our reading and teaching there of and within.

James 5:15

And the prayer of faith shall save the sick, and the Lord shall raise him up; and if he have committed sins, they shall be forgiven him.

Let's not make the mistake of using forgiveness from various pragmatic viewpoints or common viewpoints as some, nor any of what the self-adorned folks call an excuse. That's all a Christian needs is another excuse. When the time comes, our souls will be required for our iniquities if repentance isn't in our hearts. We must decide which side of the coin, do we want to be on.

How does it all begin? Not to be killed with boredom, but for clarity and background, so you too will be well informed as to the knowledge of living a lie, I'll pour out a great deal of me, the average child from Opelousas, Louisiana. I'm the brother of four sibling brothers known at that time, and the son of a single mother and deceased father. My father died when I was four years old, but this is not your typical type of everyday jargon that you hear about, oh my daddy died and that's my excuse. No, on the contrary, I'll tell you the truth about the entire eye-opening situation.

My father was a womanizer, whoremonger, drinker, smoker, diligent provider, and self-demised man. Directly related to the history is the story of the woman that called my mother on the telephone and gave her this message, "You need to go to the hospital and see about your husband, that nigger done laid up on me in here and had a stroke." I can't explain my father's behavior, and I won't try to, and I'm not running him down. He is waiting for his reward and I still have to earn mine. The more I tried to come to grips with it, was the more I succumbed to mitigated, psychological heresies.

At the hospital, he was able to grasp my mother's hand and say I'm sorry. My mother's reply was "Don't worry about that now." Maybe she could respond in that manner, because her first two children were born out of wedlock and she didn't even know the name of the second son's father. Later you'll learn that, that child became a crack addict and committed suicide. Yes, my mother had her promiscuous moments with her frolicking adventures with whatever, and remember she said, <u>"once an adulterer always an adulterer."</u> My father had a second stroke which killed him. I was four years old at the time and my brothers basically were all four years apart in age.

GOD KNOWS YOUR NAME!

I see things dealing with children today, and the various problems that they're faced with and I think about how my older brothers perishing at a young age with the weight of the world riding and beating on them. Children need a healthy balance of spirit and flesh in their lives. This balance will assist with the tug between in the world and of the world. Parents, be cognizant of the healthy balance of spirit and flesh. Raise and rear your children but remember they want and need affection as well.

Romans 12:1-3

I beseech you therefore, brethren, by the mercies of God, that ye present your bodies a living sacrifice, holy, acceptable unto God, which is your reasonable service. **2** And be not conformed to this world: but be ye transformed by the renewing of your mind, that ye may prove what is that good, and acceptable, and perfect, will of God. **3** For I say, through the grace given unto me, to every man that is among you, not to think of himself more highly than he ought to think; but to think soberly, according as God hath dealt to every man the measure of faith.

I pray that through my eyes and voice that God's presence is known in good times and in bad times. I never provoked my children, but they were caught in the adult mess that I made for myself in complicity with their mothers. It was extremely difficult for me to provide the balance that they deserved and quite frankly needed. When we provide the precious balance between spirit and flesh, their departure from the scripture or Word of God is temporary in nature and not heavenly devastating.

Proverbs 22:6

Train up a child in the way he should go: and when he is old, he will not depart from it.

Sometimes I ask the question, why hasn't anyone ever asked me HOW LONG DOES IT TAKE? Asking that question, when it concerned my children aroused my thoughts as it pertains to family history and the generations involved. At a certain point in life, they have to fend for themselves and it's never too late to introduce God and the χριστιανός way to them. Never miss the opportunity to make The Holy Spirit ingratiating and inviting to them for in that domain they'll find peace and rest. Just stay with me, I'm sure the answer to the above question will be revealed.

HOW LONG DOES IT TAKE? How long does it take was a question that I couldn't get away from and it continued to be unanswered in my daily living? Now I wanted sex to feed and add to my errant behavior. Peer pressure added to fueling and fanning the flames of sexual encounters. Freshly fourteen years old with my sexual encounter notched in my belt, I vainly lived into a sexual direction. If a female says no after forty-five minutes of sexual intercourse and she has orgasmed then the male's orgasm is 50 percent completed, is that rape?

Before I could get the question completely out of my mouth my wife, Laura, being the rape and victim counselor that she is said "yes it is." We just don't think about such issues as we pursue the desires or purposes in life. As a corrections officer in Seattle Washington at King County Corrections Facility for 12 years, I often came in contact with inmates that had to face serious charges for just being in the wrong place at the right time or is that the right place at the wrong time. Whichever is the case, they suffered incarceration for the issue. Back to the **CHRISTIAN LIVING LIE** and the question how long does it take is still unanswered.

My mother's house with four sons was the rendezvous sex palace. It was the place where the neighborhood was saturated and subdued with curious teenage boys and girls exploring and fulfilling their sexual inquisitiveness. The truth in this topic is so personal and scary that we flee at warp speeds from revealing it. Don't overlook the other awful behaviors that's about to take place. The grace of GOD shreds the snare of the enemy.

Some of these stories have been taken to the grave, because a life of immoral and carnal acts is a life that GOD doesn't allow to live on! My mother working sixteen hours a day more often than not, aided in me activating the Roy Andrus Sr. that I vowed not to be at his grave side. The house where miscarriages and abortions were created was 113 C. Alley.

I visited the resting place of my father's body until approximately the age of thirty-eight. My mother asked me, "why are you looking for something in the dead that you ought to seek from the living," the living God that is? How long does it take? While at the side of his tomb, I would think of and desire my father to be here leading, guiding, loving and encouraging me. I realized that even if he were here that wouldn't be the case!!! You see, when your father procreates multiple children with multiple women at the same time, you don't have the time or the means to be a real father, a real man.

Matthew 8:21-23

21 And another of his disciples said unto him, Lord, suffer me first to go and bury my father. **22** But Jesus said unto him, **Follow me; and let the dead bury their dead.** **23** And when he was entered into a ship, his disciples followed him.

I would say to the grave and the bones lying there, I'm trying my best to care for my mother and I don't want to and will not make the same mistakes you made. Sex, drugs, alcohol, philandering, gambling, sodomy, stealing, suicide, adultery and depression not in the grave but living and armed for the task! Yes, the delivered me lived as he did, if not worse.

You see, I didn't want the sin to be generational, but at the beginning part of thirteen years of age I began indulging and satisfying my lust and flesh with the pleasure of multiple young women, drinking, dope smoking, stealing, gambling and a hint of violence. Had it not been for miscarriages and abortions, I would have been a father, **NO**, I would have fostered a child or children early in my teenage life.

I'd become the exact thing that I despised and vowed not to become. Hypocritically having sexual prowess with grown women that knew my father sexually and I assume they remembered the sexual pleasure that my father gave them, so they sought after it with me, a child on a moped. Every pinch on the cheek isn't as innocent as it seems. Once you have dipped your soul into the lust of the flesh, the lust of the eye, and the pride of life, turning back or remembering what you despised is not primary to your actions. I cursed and cried at my father's resting place, because in me he lived. You'll stop living that lie when you get to know your Heavenly Father!

1 John 2:15-17

[15] Love not the world, neither the things that are in the world. If any man love the world, the love of the Father is not in him. [16] For all that is in the world, the lust of the flesh, and the lust of the eyes, and the pride of life, is not of the Father, but is of the world. [17] And the world

passeth away, and the lust thereof: but he that doeth the will of God abideth for ever.

A picture was taken at my father's funeral. The picture showed a young mother standing over a casket with five children, all boys. Not unusual at all in a sinful world, but troubling none-the-less. Some might say par for the course, dismissing the obvious outcome as a black man's predetermined faith. Well, what you didn't see in the picture is determination and striation. I'm speaking of the picture of my mother and me with my four known siblings at the time, standing over the open casket that my daddy laid in after his death.

What was his legacy? Did he leave a God ordained inheritance? Oh, he left an inheritance, and you can see it in all of the relationships, failed marriages, unwedded children, suicides and drug addict issues all found in my daddy's children, both wedded and unwedded. It's a depressing situation and thus I cried in that depression in my childhood ages. Pray for the dismantling of depression and find our heavenly Father, GOD. Our arrival at that point, Jehovah, Father, God, is the inheritance that matters. We'll be better served if we choose arrival over the darkness in our travels.

Chapter 6: How We Get There

It was difficult for an eighth grade, uneducated black woman to raise and rear five boys in the 50's, 60's, 70's and 80's. She did, however be it, teach us to work hard and to be responsible. We also had a village to help raise us. My grandmother, Clemonce Broussard Richardson, often shared her knowledge and wisdom with me. A friend of mine would also let me know that a warning comes before the destruction, but I failed with precision to ignore all warnings.

We were all Christians, stood before the church, proclaiming our determination to make it to heaven and desiring each and every one to pray for us. We should have saved our oxygen. Christians force other Christians to be Christians. Meaning watch what I do and say what I say. Now Christians have fallen off into denominations and groups. It'll be interesting to see where all of these Christian socials lead to. HOW LONG DOES IT TAKE? Thank you, Mama, for raising us in the ways of the Lord!!!

Hope was gone and reckless living seemed to be the only way for me. When I was 9 or 10 years old, my mother asked me to go to the store and buy some ice scream. I became upset for no satisfactory reason and snatched the money out of her hand jumped on my bicycle riding and roaring in anger and I failed to stop at the intersection of C. Alley and Market St. I was struck by a car thrown in the air and landed uninjured. That was my first brush with death. Three people witnessed that moment and they couldn't believe that I had suffered not one scratch from that car striking me. This looks like warning and destruction with God stepping in. I can tell you now that I cried for years as a child when I thought about the father that I didn't have. That day I had thoughts of him on my mind and I didn't cry anymore, but I just acted out. HOW LONG DOES IT TAKE?

  Indulgence felt great to me. I ignored all of the warnings before my indulgences defied and disobeyed the guidance of the village that raised me, even when it cost me flesh and pain. I'm speaking about the flesh and pain spurned by the discipline of my mother. If we are committed to the depravity and wickedness that is disruptive and destructive, then we must pay the penalty or toll that is incumbent of such abominate actions and atrocities. The toll and penalty for our effervescence and

Christian manners shall be realized on a heavenly scale for the wrath of God is far greater than the wrath of our parents or the village. What has to occur for us to take a different path to the understanding of God's plan of salvation?

Ezekiel 33:10-12

[10] Therefore, O thou son of man, speak unto the house of Israel; Thus ye speak, saying, If our transgressions and our sins be upon us, and we pine away in them, how should we then live? [11] Say unto them, As I live, saith the Lord God, I have no pleasure in the death of the wicked; but that the wicked turn from his way and live: turn ye, turn ye from your evil ways; for why will ye die, O house of Israel? [12] Therefore, thou son of man, say unto the children of thy people, The righteousness of the righteous shall not deliver him in the day of his transgression: as for the wickedness of the wicked, he shall not fall thereby in the day that he turneth from his wickedness; neither shall the righteous be able to live for his righteousness in the day that he sinneth.

Stealing candy was the first indulgence, but I got caught and my older brother answered the phone when they called the house. He bailed me out of that, because he was very tall and they thought he was my father. Thanks Reggie, love you much Bro! Stealing roosters with Walter bought another brush with death as one night the police responded which led to a nervous white policeman shaking and pointing a gun at us. We got caught, because I wanted to burn a spider web and not leave after we secured the roosters. Walter's quick tongue got us out of that jam which led to a ride home from the police versus us being shot and killed for stealing roosters.

GOD KNOWS YOUR NAME!

I can't imagine the beating I would've received if Mama knew that I started stealing her car at the age of 15. Replacing the gas, making sure the contents were placed exactly where she left them and parking the car exactly where she parked it was all that entailed. The law calls it; Taking A Motor Vehicle Without Permission. My mother never knew that I was a thief, and therefore; it didn't cost me any flesh, blood, or pain. Evelyn whipped and beat with an extension cord with brutal corrective intensions and the cost was flesh, blood, and pain. Let me stay at this age for a minute.

I was gambling shooting a game of 4 ball pool against a man twice my age for $2.00 per game at

2:30am in the Red Carpet Lounge in Opelousas one morning. After losing 5 games the man refused to pay me the $2.00 that he owed me. I went up front and told the owner that the man had lost, and he's refusing to pay me. She reached behind the bar and grabbed a .38 caliber hand gun (pistol) and said "come on follow me." When we returned to the billiard room, she asked me to point the man out. She approached the man with the weapon and held it inches from his head and demanded that he pay me the $2.00 that he owed me.

    The gentleman threw the $2.00 on the pool table and then she said to him "now getcho ass outta here and don't come back." Just being a teenage gambler and almost got some one killed over $2.00. The simplest of sin goes far beyond our expectancy in the most trivial of times. Even darker to the topic is the fact that the man almost lost his life for a $2.00 gambling debt. If there's any doubt to the story, just ask anyone in Opelousas if the owner of the Red Carpet Lounge on Market St. was serious about shooting that gentleman for trying to cheat me out of my money in her club. A murder for $2.00 back then is a murder for looking the wrong way these days.

In my teenage years, I had a gun pointed at me on two occasions with the intent to end me, so I know what that gentleman must have been feeling and thinking at that moment. In my second moment, I stepped in front of a gun being pointed at my best friend by a man in his thirties. It occurred because of a short conversation between my best friend and the girl friend of the older gentleman, and by the way, she was in her thirties as well. We were playing pinball at one of our spots when the conversation took place. She took too long to return to the car, so the boyfriend was irritated and fuming. Staring at that gun and talking him down had me in two mental positions that I never cared to be in ever again!

For those of you that are questioning where is my mother during this time in my early teens, the answer is that she was in a medication induced sleep. She had been prescribed medication to help her deal with her physical and mental issues. So, just about every evening around 9pm I roamed and delighted myself in the pleasures of flesh. It was financed by the money that I earned delivering the Daily World Newspaper. That money supported my drinking, gambling, doping, whoring, and playing. This is how we get there. This is how a thirteen-year-old boy gets guns pointed at him and a fourteen-year-old boy gets girls pregnant. How we get there? How we get there?

Starting at 13 years of age, drinking alcohol seemed to be a mainstay in my life. If those around me drank I drank. Hell, even if those around me didn't drink, I still drank. Drinking never really did anything for me. Clearly from my personality and charismatic actions, I didn't need to drink to have a great time. I wasn't a dark hearted person. What was this drinking all about? To start at such an early age is indicative of background, circumstances and supervision, such as, single working parent, following the older sibling examples or even peer pressures.

We can't rule out ignorance and just a sheer desire to do wrong. Drinking seemed to be the catalyst to a multitude and plethora of flesh feeding, disruptive behavior. Every time that I and Tuckina had sex, I was drunk. I wasn't always drunk or high when doing wrong, but doing wrong was usually second nature after drinking and getting high. Acts of gambling, sex, violence and disrespect for people's space and concerns were just the tip of the iceberg.

One early morning during my high school days myself, Walter, and JayMack were cruising around in various places and towns drinking and getting high weed smoking as we usually did, when JayMack uttered to Walter, "man watch that car in front us," and Walter replied "I got it" then moments later the tires screech and a crash and bang followed. The gentleman that we hit looked at his car and saw no damage, so he asked if we were okay and then he left. JayMack's grandmother's car, the car that we were riding in, was mangled, but drivable.

GOD KNOWS YOUR NAME!

We drove around for a few more hours getting higher and drunker while JayMack tried to come up with an excuse for the damages to his grandmother's car. I began to laugh in the back seat and couldn't stop laughing, so much so, that they almost had to bring me to the ER. What do you become when you lose touch with reality? I got it JayMack yelled out.

I'll park the car in the street when I get home and blame it on a hit and run when they notice the damages in the morning. Believe it or not, a police report was filed and a search for a hit and run suspect ensued. JayMack died at an early age. To his detriment and demise, the flesh never let go of the strangle hold it had on him. Parents, please stop giving your children too much leeway and credit, especially if you weren't there to witness what occurred. Always remember the question how long does it take.

In those days, drinking and driving also garnered me a DWI at the age of fifteen. I traded my moped for Shortie's car. He was the boyfriend of Tuckina's older sister. Naturally, I called Walter and we rolled while downing a case of Old English beer. Speeding got the State Police behind us and the arrest led to my mother calling in favors to get the incident dismissed. That dismissal didn't stop me nor did it deter me. Do you remember what was said and proclaimed at my visits to my father's grave? Don't write a check with your mouth that your actions can't cash! How long does it take?

Life comes in cycles and it's important to solidify and maintain positive cycles! The one cycle that was the most positive for my family was the presence and teaching of the church. My mother was excellent and a champion at making sure that we were found in church and in the ways of the Lord, however; when you think it's enough, think again. Suicide, sex, gambling, sodomy, violence, depression, children out of wedlock, divorce, stealing, drugs and alcohol played crucial parts in the lives of all my mother's children. We had a failure to follow instructions. We have to follow the instructions if we want to remain superior over evil.

Not to place blame on my dead father, but anything has to start somewhere. If you want to go down that gofer hole, you may want to begin at my great, great, grandfather, a white man, sleeping with his white wife, white women and black slaves and black women. That bit of information came from my grandmother, Emma Guidry Andrus. One day, I was intelligent enough to recognize and question the cycle.

Why has drugs, sex, alcohol, sodomy, stealing, children out of wedlock, violence, depression, divorce, thoughts of suicide, gambling and prison been such a force in the disruption of our Christian lives? As adult χριστιανóςs, we don't get to use generational ties or history as a scapegoat for our iniquity and transgression performances. We can act abysmal and foolish trying to marginalize our past behavior, but God is keeping an accurate account.

1 John 2:16

For all that is in the world, the lust of the flesh, and the lust of the eyes, and the pride of life, is not of the Father, but is of the world.

We get there because of motive and opportunity. The motive is the lust that we inherently carry in our hearts and spirits. Such has been the crippling factor of humankind for a great season. At best, we can look for the silver lining without expectation. Once humankind has reached this state of mind of physical and mental pleasures, not much can be said or done to remove or delete this appetite. Opportunity after opportunity will avail itself. Hind sight shows it as a feeding frenzy fueled by an energetic passion that causes Lucifer Himself to explode with jubilee and honor! How do we get there? **CHOICE**

There were relatives, aunts, adults, and cousins, that witnessed this Christian child's behavior and they never said a word to my mother. Would witnessed sodomy and miscarriages be enough to compel them to inform my mother of what was occurring? I would venture to say no it wouldn't. Can you see the coming and arrival of my false sensitivity. Bred by father and mother to fulfill the commandments, but allowed to roam to and fro. Left, unknowingly, to make hell bound choices at a very early age. Watch for the signs and symptoms because they were definitely there!!!

Chapter 7: Released from the Leash

I was armed with the upbringing of a good Christian child. Yes sir, no sir, yes ma'am, no ma'am, opening and holding doors, picking up dropped items, propensity, patience, persistence, time, nothing to lose and the sly smile that captivated while plunging the dagger. I know now that all of my Christian upbringing and rearing, was the it factors, that kept so many women hanging in there under the unspoken hope and false pretense that my love and heart would belong only to them. If you couldn't picture man as a snake, you better recognize. I had been at it since thirteen, and as in anything you apply yourself to you seem to develop a skill set or trade craft.

Yeah, that good Christian upbringing, along with effervescence and charisma, came in handy in most sexual situations and sufficed for many of my adult years as well. The wu (dialects) and smile of a Christian is dangerous! It gave power and the thought of conviction to girls and women who didn't know how dangerous and reckless I truly was! Watch out for the innocent, because they're guilty as hell. This is the start of behavior and acts that were so vain and uncaring that I eventually started to call women by the wrong name, such as; Burteen called Facera.

I'm teaching, so pay close attention. When you're having a conversation or disagreement with someone and they call you the wrong name, *take a step back*. During sexual intercourse if someone calls you the wrong name, *take a step back*. Do not let that occurrence go unchecked or abolished. These moments are at the pinnacle of a relationship or commitment and to be thinking or infatuated with something or someone else is disturbing, dangerous and shattering. Now would be a great time for you to pay close attention to the χριστιανός revelation. Whatever you do, don't fall for the flimsy excuse that's about to follow the behavior. I don't want to be the one to say I told you so. Back to more of me now.

My release from the leash of Mama and Opelousas came at the age of seventeen. I decided to attend The DeVry Institute of Technology in Irving, Texas two weeks after I graduated from Opelousas High School. Earlier I indicated that Satan had taught and configured me in all that he wanted out of me, but at this point, I'm about to become lethal. He would dispatch one woman on my second day at school. It's difficult to look at ourselves from the inside, meaning spiritually looking. The second day, really! I'm backing off the virtual and visual information, but you know from the Chapter Title what I'm trying to share with you and protect you from.

When I moved out of my mother's house, I found myself, a country boy, in the big city of Dallas, Texas seventeen years of age and a Christian. Now I could have a variety of women, women of different races, ethnicities, cultures and motives with the way paved for my drinking, dope smoking and my **CHRISTIAN LIVING LIE**. Women in the big city taught me more about destructive sexual behavior including anal and oral sex with the use of sex toys and mechanisms. We definitely have a failure to follow instructions at this point. Mama didn't send me there for that.

Meanwhile, back in Louisiana someone was holding on for that amazing future with me and she loved me so, that I thought I was a god (careful)!!!

Exodus 20:1-3

And God spake all these words, saying, [2] I am the Lord thy God, which have brought thee out of the land of

Egypt, out of the house of bondage. ³ Thou shalt have no other gods before me.

Ladies ask yourselves the question, why. Why do you allow such disrespect and aimless actions to control and deter your ability to move forward in righteousness? I'm begging you to stop being so vulnerable and preyed upon. You can avoid and stop the madness with the power of your choice.

Young ladies and women stop living beneath you, and please hold men accountable, and don't fall victim to this type of abuse. A man like me at that point in life was only capable of dragging women through the mud with my mild manners and good work ethic. This ain't no romance novel and it sure isn't a blue print or model for good behavior. Stay with me, because I'm sure you'll be able to avoid the messy spiritual bumps and hurdles in life from the knowledge of my Christian antics. <u>*Christian men often make love to a woman without loving the woman and chances are she fell for him.*</u> You've heard it from the Pastor now make men accountable or keep letting them wreak havoc in your life and emotion stability.

We should be very careful not to tempt or play with God.

Numbers 14:21-23

²¹ But as truly as I live, all the earth shall be filled with the glory of the Lord. ²² Because all those men which have seen my glory, and my miracles, which I did in Egypt and in the wilderness, and have tempted me now these ten times, and have not hearkened to my voice; ²³ Surely they shall not see the land which I sware unto their fathers, neither shall any of them that provoked me see it:

I must say that due to the brushes with death that I've encounter at such an early age. I've never been one to provoke, but it seemed to not matter when I lived in the darkness of life. Death from carnality is inevitable, but our behavior can cause annals of time to be our present time. At this point, we need those prayers that have been prayed long ago because we just can't seem to fly straight.

The newspaper route in Opelousas has been left behind, but I managed to find three jobs while I was attending school. Somewhat as my father, Roy, I worked hard, but played harder! The multitude of my **CHRISTIAN LIVING** behavior would not be hampered by the obligation of school and three jobs. The ferocious spirit of indulgence and flesh just feeds and nurtures itself with the passing of everyday. I heard the rapper say in his lyrics that money, sex, and success was all that he was feeling and living. I just revealed and shared the spot light of Christianity with you. I don't know if the rapper was a Christian or not, but his mother did a great deal of praying for him.

No mother, no village, and no boundaries was the truth, but the monthly phone calls home never spoke that truth. If truth had been told then, how could I continue to live the Christian lie? Then how could I live out the adversary's plan and entanglement of me? Remember the title of the book. From the title, it's very clear that we live multiple lives within our life. None more prevalent than the Christian lie. If we could pull back layers as with sheets and towels, the exposure would be frightening.

How do we approach the issue of this **CHRISTIAN LIVING LIE**? You can't hold your children's hands 24/7, but you can teach and prepare them for life's experiences.

Deuteronomy 6:4 -9

⁴ Hear, O Israel: The Lord our God is one Lord: ⁵ And thou shalt love the Lord thy God with all thine heart, and with all thy soul, and with all thy might. ⁶ And these words, which I command thee this day, shall be in thine heart: ⁷

And thou shalt teach them diligently unto thy children, and shalt talk of them when thou sittest in thine house, and when thou walkest by the way, and when thou liest down, and when thou risest up. ⁸ And thou shalt bind them for a sign upon thine hand, and they shall be as frontlets between thine eyes. ⁹ And thou shalt write them upon the posts of thy house, and on thy gates.

Praying for them is the ultimate cover. You'll see this scripture again, because it's extremely important. Some years later I would lose my affinity for gambling on the pool table because of a brawl in a pool hall that a friend of mine was in and someone fractured his skull with a pool cue. We don't know what it will take for us to change our wrong doings, but we will change. I was recently released from the leash so change wasn't in the approach just yet.

In the big city, I learned that it takes showers and weeks to wash some women off of you. I learned more about sex and sexual acts that when coupled with my Christian life, and fraudulent Christian appearance, I literally became lethal. Believe it, we can cause other folks to suffer from depression! Christian upbringing and work ethic is a façade at this point. It only created hurt and disbelief when emotion or feelings were involved. At work or sports, it vowed well.

Listen, when a woman truly gave herself to me, I mean really let go and disregarded all warnings and negative possibilities and gave her heart to me and my foolishness, I relished in the power and control given to me, and it pleased Satan so much, because he knew that he had a great instrument in lust and conquering!!! The question, why do we give others such power and dominion over our journey, needs to be critically and spiritually answered and we need the presence of guidance and positive, advantageous, and enduring choice. The Holy Spirit is more than a diversion. It's mystical and wondrous not self-serving and serves those who seek His content.

Because of errant behavior I failed major courses in the eleventh grade and had to repeat them in the twelfth grade in order to graduate. This same ignorance accompanied me in Texas when I was seventeen years of age. I lived in an apartment complex with a real, life Cheech and Chong guy name Juan and a bunch of college kids that always had a pool party going on. I dove right in and Juan's dope made me higher and more inebriated than I had ever been! Thank God that I didn't chase or depend on the high. I also had a Hispanic homosexual roommate. No, I didn't have a sexual encounter with my roommate. Eknard the Hispanic homosexual and the good Christian boy from Louisiana were roommates. Talk about a culture shock! He had a good heart and he cared about people, although he had to deal with an abundance of harassment and scrutiny. The stigmatism of homosexuality magically rubbing off on you was the thought in that day. Neither I nor any of my brothers are homosexual, are on the down low, but we have children that are a part of the LBGTQ community. Ignorance hurts those around us and we should make a valiant effort to not stigmatize but to love.

I want to offer sincere and heartfelt thanks to Linda Prow, and Phil Derrick. God placed you right where you needed to be when I needed y'all to be there and I'm sure many lives were touched and blessed by y'all's presence and position at DeVry Institute of Technology in Irving Texas! Again, thank you so much for all that you did for me!

This is a tell all opportunity and by telling all I intend to support, change, and enlighten the masses by shedding a sincere light on what *From Christian to χριστιανός* means. If sin was the end, I would be toast. If folk would've tried me by the spirit fire of the Lord, they would've beheaded the insurrection of the threat to their comprehension of a real man and the stability in knowing what one feels, looks, and acts like.

Partying, working three jobs and being a fulltime student led me on a collision course with failure. Older gentlemen would use the phrase, burning the candle at both ends, to describe my behavior. I did give some thought to what I wanted to be or achieve in life when I would become a responsible member of society. Policeman, Electronic Technician or Military were the career choices and not necessarily in that order.

Being too young to be a policeman led me to Irving, Texas at DeVry Institute of Technology where I would begin studies on becoming an electronic technician, the sex slave to Buaniti, the school security officer, and an out of place country child that was taught to carry his Christian teachings everywhere and, in most cases, let it precede me in all circumstances. If you've ever heard the phrase kindness kills, believe it. Buaniti didn't care about my kindness or my Christian appearance. She was only interested in taking me through sexual indulgences that you don't get explained from your parents or sex education class. The kind of sexual indulgences that had three or four people being involved was the norm and no act was off limits. I was so enamored with what she was teaching me at that point, I couldn't wait to infiltrate the high rise buildings and the sophisticated scene. From my activities, a rich woman from Montana was dropping out of school and wanted me to follow her. She said that I wouldn't have to worry, because her family was rich.

Then a phone call had to be made home, where I would have to ensure my mother that I was living the Christian life that she had spent the majority of my life teaching me to live. Of course, I left out the part about _no guidance and bad choices. How long does it take?_ Do you know? We abandon the truth at all opportunistic moments, but we let obedient and prosperous opportunities in the goodness of the Lord dwindle and escape our attention.

After I flunked out of school, I continued to work and live in Dallas, Texas with my cousin Russell. Thanks, cuz for your contribution that has culminated into now. Prior to me moving in with him, I had gone to the Army recruiter and enlisted in the military on the delayed entry program. I had taken the test, ASVAB, to enter the military while I was in High School. I played chicken scratch with it not knowing that the test would determine what branch of service I could enter and the job I could qualify to do. Being the Christian that I was, I stayed in contact with Buaniti if you know what I mean. Only the blood of Jesus washes us clean, but I lived outside of that knowledge and forged a way for increasing sinful behavior. Behavior that we omit counting the cost for because it defies all logic and truth.

While living with my cousin, multiple women came from out of town to be with me. I also had Tuckina in Opelousas that loved and was waiting for me. She cherished the ground that I walked on, in spite of being pounded on by her mother warning of my presumed stature as the good Christian man. As the time neared for me to embark on my military experience, I rented a car and made my way home to visit and say my goodbyes. That process of goodbyes would happen on an abundance of occasions from city to city, ocean to ocean, state to state and continent to continent. My false sensitivity and shallow emotional content for people and what they were experiencing hadn't yet been exposed. My intellect and splendor were beginning to flourish. My stern and confident presence forged on a different path. **GOD KNOWS YOUR NAME!**

Chapter 8: The Military Adult Christian

The older women in Opelousas were impressed with what Buaniti had taught me, but the girl that I was supposed to be in love with, that wore my engagement ring and cherished the ground that I walked on didn't react as they did!! After teaching her how to orally please me and put her in several different sexual positions, she knew that I had been unfaithful and promiscuous. Promiscuity wasn't anything new for me, but Buaniti performed her devilish work on me and I transported the devil sexually as best as I could. I tortured Tuckina's spirit and she could no longer recognize the Christian that she thought I was. She removed the engagement ring from her finger and threw it at me while leaving my presence crying and screaming. Of course, I continued to mislead her in the years that followed and twenty years later we spent some time together to see if we could recreate our teenage love.

<u>Young ladies and women stop living beneath you and please hold men accountable, and don't fall victim to this type of abuse</u>. I can't stress that

enough! Let me repeat something that I said earlier, a man like me at that point in life was only capable of dragging women through the mud. The promiscuity was still there in her mind, thoughts and feelings. I, Marvin the Christian, was capable of that and stripping people of their control and choice with my flawed Christian character and false solid commitments.

Upon my return trip to Dallas, I fell asleep behind the wheel while driving on the Interstate. When I awakened, I had crossed over into the median and was about to slam into a pylon holding up an overpass. I swerved and over corrected and the car went back across the Interstate into oncoming traffic narrowly missing other cars and cars narrowly missed me. **GOD STEPPING IN.** That would be my continued brush with death.

Would that change me or my Christian behavior? I think not. Another drink or hit of dope would be the remedy of choice for me. Somehow, we always seem to choose the un-sound methods or solutions. Did I mention that I and my oldest brother ran off the road and into a huge ditch going to Arnaudville, Louisiana in that same car just four days prior? When *Jehovah* is talking, it would behoove folks to listen and act accordingly!!! χριστιανός don't have a problem with that.

GOD KNOWS YOUR NAME!

The Army fit me like a glove and I was a great prospect to the Army. I really regretted not applying myself when I took the ASVAB Test instead of playing chicken scratch. Fortunately, I was able to retake it while I was in the Army and I improved on all of my scores which opened a few doors for my military career. Unfortunately, at Ft. Hood Texas my second duty station, I found the dope crowd, and the pleasure and promiscuity of Wendy from Georgia. Wendy from Georgia, was an Army Reserve Nurse. She came to Opelousas un-announced and you'll hear more about that later.

God gave me another chance. My Platoon Sergeant told me to stop the ignorant stuff just before they gave me a look or test me for my awful behavior. GOD STEPPING IN. SSG Hitchcock, thank you for choosing my good over my bad, and seeing the best in me. I pray that God has covered you by the blood of Jesus as you covered me in that instance.

For three days prior to the test, I ingested bottles of B-12 vitamins, pints of Black Velvet alcohol, and cases of beer all in efforts to clear my system of the stuff and it worked. That was probably the longest 4 days in my life. I tried to warn the other soldiers about them knowing that we were doing stuff and they didn't listen to me. They were tested the same day that I was and the results weren't good. Somehow, even after I went to them to warn them, I became a snitch. If a choice had to be made between being a snitch, and an opportunity to change my life altering issues, I'll take the snitch comments.

I received a promotion shortly thereafter and was sent to Camp Stanton, Korea for a duty station. I never touched drugs or dope again after that. Guidance and choice powered me past the doom. Wow, all of this has occurred and I haven't turned nineteen yet!!! I took advantage of my second chance to be a good soldier one that my peers and fellow soldiers could count on. Listen to me, watch what God can do!!!

I saw a media presentation of a young man, a former college football player that had lost the use of his right arm, and nearly died after he made a tackle in a football game. His speech was so powerful and authentic. The focus and purpose of the lecture was to impact, inspire and empower those persons in attendance to remain goal oriented and to realize the attainability of their goals.

The most powerful thing that he said was "don't give up." Life after several disastrous, indulgent and impulsive decisions will surely impact your ability and desire to be your best olympic person and soldier for the Lord. God prepares and sustains us in our goal to labor for Him and to love Him. In God, we'll find the ability to authentically impact, inspire and empower His children.

Romans 8:14

For as many as are led by the Spirit of God, they are the sons of God.

I recall a couple of tragic incidents occurring in the eleven months that I was stationed at Ft. Hood, Texas. While on a two-week field exercise involving multiple units several hundred soldiers with lots of vehicles and equipment, a soldier near our camp or position was sleeping in his sleeping bag in the early hours of the morning and he was run over by a tank. There was nothing left of him that was identifiable.

On another field exercise, our unit with a few other units was on a field exercise that involved training us in our secondary job as infantry soldiers. The weather was extremely bad. The rain was coming down hard visibility was poor, and it had rained for a few days. Our unit and support unit received a mission to get to a certain location and provide ground support for a field artillery unit approximately seven kilometers away, if memory serves me correct. The military always moves under the cover of darkness.

The route that we took was to lead us into an ambush that was conducted by other units that were participating in the exercise. The attacking unit was supposed to find the prime location in our route to initiate the ambush and they found the perfect location! They set up the ambush on both sides of the road from a higher elevation after crossing a small bridge. As half of our unit got across the bridge, they began their assault. Smoke grenades, M60 and M16 fire poured down on us. It was only blanks people, but that was the beginning of **_nobody wins in a war and war changes a man._**

In natural reaction to take cover from the attack not realizing or comprehending the level and fervent flow of the water in the stream under the bridge, a hand full of our soldiers jumped in the stream and was immediately swept away by the current. Four soldiers drowned that night and the question of "when" came to my thoughts. When? In my Christian thoughts, I wondered when my careless and reckless behavior is going to catch up with me. Stigmatized by frantic aimless running around, with what or nothing as an end, is counterproductive to and for a χριστιανός. How long does it take? The question still remains.

My second night in Korea 1985, my fellow soldiers took me on a traditional thunder run. On the thunder run, you stop at every bar and club in multiple towns and you have one drink or beer. We did three towns and about nine taxi rides that night and we only had a few hours to recover before reporting for duty the next day. Promiscuity followed me to Korea. In fact, promiscuity followed me everywhere I traveled.

On two separate occasions, I had to go to the clinic for treatment for a sexually transmitted disease called Chlamydia. That news could've been worst, i.e. aids, cancroids, herpes, syphilis, but God gave me more chances in the absence of guidance and choice. GOD STEPPING IN. We are afforded quite a few spiritual entitlements in life, but none more, greater than love and chance. In the eleven months that I served in Korea, God found favor in me.

GOD KNOWS YOUR NAME!

Every project, competition, situation and employment that I committed my focus, attention, and effort I excelled and achieved awesome success. As I went along my way, my character and mild manners garnered me respect and trust amongst my associates and peers. The commitment of my heart and spirit was impossible. Some Christians would say that the favor of God was over me, but I feel that His favor was on borrowed time. The heart and spirit are where we congregate with the purpose of God and I was non-committal. My existence was based on pleasing and satisfying flesh. I was falling for the right thing and standing for the wrong thing. Consult the guidance of the Holy Spirit and make a committed choice.

I received two promotions and an additional promotable status to become a leader. God put

Captains Frost and Burnette and 1st Sergeant Calvin Spencer Jr. in my life. These men saw the work ethic in me that had been instilled in me by my mother and those that had a part in raising me, such as; grandmothers, ear pulling church ushers, and the stay-at-home moms of the neighborhood. They prepared, sent, and used me for every competition and board that I could participate in and I didn't let them down. The victories and wins just kept coming in. It would've been awesome if I could've claimed that for Christ.

In between the great things, I managed to receive an overnight pass one evening. The pass started when you got off duty and expired at 4:30am the following morning. I got into a stupid argument with my girlfriend, of which I can't remember about, and I left the club where she worked and went to another club on the other side of town. I drank and drank some more and drank some more until I left with a club girl. I did what I left the club with her to do, which was to send my girlfriend the message that the other side of town exist.

I over slept and missed my return time to Camp Stanton. The First Sergeant and the Captain had to notify the General that I hadn't returned from my overnight pass, but they hadn't started to search for me at that point. The First Sergeant summoned my best friend at the time to his office and told him to log out a vehicle with another soldier and go find me because he knew where I was. *This is something interesting!* I wasn't where Jordan knew I was suppose to be, but my girlfriend knew where I was and where I had spent the night. She directed him right to the front door. HOW?

Jordan knocked on the door and I opened my eyes. When I saw the daylight, I knew that I was in the wrong place and that I had missed my curfew. I open my every morning now with thanks for God in my spirit, heart, and mind. On the ride back, Jordan and I would talk about how upset the First Sergeant was. I really wanted to turn the jeep around and go the other way. If y'all knew First Sergeant Calvin Spencer Jr. like I knew him, you would understand. He said, "the Captain wanted to issue me an Article Fifteen write-up for Dereliction of Duty", but he told the Captain that he would give me a choice of the Article Fifteen or what he had for my punishment. Article Fifteens and disciplinary issues end careers, so I chose the punishment that he had for me. For 45 days, my day didn't end until 8pm. For 90 days, my movement was restricted to the dining facility, the motor pool, the Captain's office, where ever I drove the Captain for that day, and the barracks.

GOD KNOWS YOUR NAME!

I survived First Sergeant Calvin Spencer Jr. and he gave me a pat on the back because he didn't think I could handle those 45 days. First Sergeant Calvin Spencer Jr. when he first introduced himself to all 180 of us, called himself "A I D S" "Ass Injected Death Syndrome". The favor of God in my accomplishments and awards came thru this man and his confidence in my abilities as a soldier!!! The point is this: It's not always what you think, hear, or see!!!

The awards and promotions just kept coming until one day at the driver of the division board and competition at a moment when the competition was mine to drive away with, the judge saw from the documents that I wore glasses, and I wasn't wearing them. I didn't have them with me. They had to send soldiers on a two hour drive to get me and the vehicle because the instructor wouldn't let me drive back to Camp Stanton. Hey you can't win them all! The First Sergeants response was, *"Andrus, I oughtta kick you in yo nutts. Now get out a ma face."*

Promiscuity and whoremongering is in full effect. I kept in touch with Tuckina, my childhood sweetheart in Opelousas, while I was in Korea letting her know how much I loved and missed her, that being a bunch of bull crap!!!!!! She never knew about the clinic visits or Wendy from Georgia that I kept in touch with as well. I had a Korean prostitute that I met shortly after my arrival in Korea. Normally, it cost sixty to seventy dollars a month for the young woman to do everything you wanted her to do, i.e. wash clothes, sex, feed and cater to me in any way I saw fit.

I used the excuse of not having any money because I sent it all home to care for my mother so I never paid a dime. However, I did spend tons of cash on drinking with my buddies and playing video games in the club. I believe the club boss and mother, the girl's owners, saw me to be the marrying type that would end up marrying Jeannie and bringing her to the United States and we all know what that leads to. I spent my last evening in Korea on a farewell thunder run with my fellow soldiers.

I managed to get intoxicated enough not to remember where I was or how I got there, but I do remember putting a hobbling Korean woman on my back and carrying her to a hooch. I woke up naked, so I assumed that I had drunken, unprotected sex with her. Do you remember those visits to my father's grave and what I proclaimed to the dead man? Well keep reading, and Wendy from Georgia may be brought up again as well.

As you can see there is an expansion occurring in my territory, and it isn't the God guided expansion prayed for as contained in Jabez's prayer.

1 Chronicles 4:9-10
[9] And Jabez was more honourable than his brethren: and his mother called his name Jabez, saying, Because I bare him with sorrow. [10] And Jabez called on the God of Israel, saying, Oh that thou wouldest bless me indeed, and enlarge my coast, and that thine hand might be with me, and that thou wouldest keep me from evil, that it may not grieve me! And God granted him that which he requested.

The military is actually assisting in increasing my territory and my indulgences. Interaction with other races and ethnicities was definitely different in other parts of the United States and the world from the southern states. If this was my moment to feel great about darkness, evil, and wickedness on a global scale, this would be a good time to broadcast my meritless accomplishment. Always remember that by our truth in prayer and faith in God, that we are superior over evil.

GOD KNOWS YOUR NAME!

Believe it or not, in this time frame I'm helping my mother and family sustain their living and I'm helping other soldiers become better soldiers. I was being the best soldier I could be for the leaders that were depending on me to remain missile and foxhole ready. My work ethic instilled in me at an early age by my mother is paying big dividends for me as a soldier. Don't knock it just try it. Life contains heavenly, visceral, and carnal advancements. We focus all of our energy, attention, and efforts on these advancements and on some occasions, we get to enjoy the fruition of our endeavors. In these endeavors, I would implore and urge you to understand the nature and the three parts of man. Search and explore the three parts of man and dig real deep.

That search will most assuredly lead us to the revelation of our plight as it relates to the direction of our efforts, energy and attention. I enjoyed the fruition of the visceral and carnal advancements from my time in Korea, but there was still something missing and I know that we all have that feeling when something is complete, but still, something is missing. Just pray and pray some more, then pray some more.

I met Wendy from Georgia, while I was stationed at Ft. Hood, the previous duty station in Texas. She satiable seduced and let me be and do everything that Buaniti had taught me while I was attending DeVry Institute 1983. Wendy must have been Buaniti's clone because she reciprocated every action with equal, conquering, mind-boggling intention. The thought of being a Christian never entered my mind during these times. This was very reckless to say the least, but true and honest talk. Remember that un-announced visit Wendy made to Opelousas. That happened days before I went to Korea. She was in Opelousas at the same time that I was supposed to be spending with Tuckina, the girl that I "loved" so much.

I called Wendy from the airport in Seattle, Washington when I returned from Korea. I told her that I was in Georgia and that I needed her to come and pick me up at the bus station. She said, "okay, but she would have to make up an excuse because she was lying next to her fiancé." I guess she intended to hide me in a hotel and sneak around town with me as I did with her when she came to Opelousas eleven months earlier. The evil that came with me satisfying flesh hurts and disturbs those close and around me to this very moment. It's like a question mark or asterisk to my living for God and my pursuit of the spirit. It's amazing to serve God and His People, no matter the doubter or hatter! Promiscuity isn't selfish or caring. It'll use and accept any of us, but *to God be the glory because that to did pass.* HOW LONG DOES IT TAKE?

Chapter 9: Time Brings About a Change

At the adolescent age of 20, I did another eleven month transfer from Camp Stanton, Korea to Ft. Lewis, Washington where God's favor and my Christian behavior continued to both bless and hinder me. God's favor never hinders so get that thought out of your mind. In eighteen months while stationed at Ft. Lewis, I earned two more promotions and a severe status elevation amongst the female hopefuls and leaches of course. Around every military base there are more than enough women desiring to receive government benefits.

Present day, men and women with jobs and benefits are prime catches. The leaches didn't get a rise out of me, but the good women, the Christian women, the working women, the women looking for a good man were the targets of my bullshit and lying Christian behind. To be promiscuous is like playing with a loaded gun and that's exactly what I was doing. HOW LONG DOES IT TAKE? So much hurt and depression were caused by living my Christian lies. What good could come out of that? We'll have to wait and see.

For my 21st birthday a friend of mine, Burks, took me out to a high-end club that was located in the Marriot Hotel in Seattle. It was named the Gambit if memory serves me correct. You probably won't believe this, but a young lady overheard that it was my birthday and bought me a long Island drink that came with the invitation to join her at her place for the evening.

I refused the drink and the invitation. Suddenly, I didn't want to drink alcohol anymore, so at that moment I quit drinking. She was gorgeous and a very sexy woman and Burks was urging me to accept her invitation to spend the evening with her at her place, but that seemed to be so reckless and endangering to me that I refused. The transgression and iniquity list just took a hit. In my actions, you should see that I made a choice. Choice is more powerful than we know.

During my time at Ft. Lewis, I chose to participate in orgies, night club fights, reckless driving at 150 mph on I-5, and having other men's wives and girlfriends. At the Trae Club, The Knife and Gun Club, on North Fort one evening as I walked around the club, a guy grabbed me by the arm and asked me a threatening question. I had my hand in my pocket on my knife.

I removed it from my pocket and opened the blade just that quick. After a moment, he said "my bad I thought you were somebody else." I came that close to committing a murder because I intended on slashing his throat. An open bladed knife that you don't stab or use on someone is another chance to change situations and circumstances. If you're at the thought that I didn't deserve the favor of God, you're probably right, but then who does? Let's see where this leads us. I'm a legally grown man now and I quit, gambling, drinking, stealing, lying, and dope smoking and it would appear that my Christian upbringing is beginning to resurface. Let's not get ahead of ourselves. I've got more marriages to get through in the narrative, so some lies were still uttered. I was approached by my friend Herv.

He said that he and his wife had meant a nice young lady through a mutual acquaintance of theirs. Her name was Sparkle and she worked at the Seattle Times. He said here I got her number for you. Herv and Dayna playing match maker, oh boy not good! Sparkle made me forget about the girlfriend, Rowita from Tonga, that I had as a girlfriend at the time. Sparkle without sex had captured and slayed parts of me that I didn't even know existed.

Do you remember me mentioning that this was an eighteen-month tour of duty? Over the course of a couple of months we bonded and I even got introduced to mom and dad. Dad was a gigantic brother from Monroe, Louisiana. Seriously, this was the first time that a woman had ever truly, without reservation received my heart, true love and affection.

Her smile, positive attitude, care for others and just her good nature melted me and bought out the good in me. I felt alive, clean, wholesome and passionate for life and she was a Christian as well. She took my heart to the next level, as it concerned emotions and feelings for a woman and then the situation changed. Just like a scratched record, a halt in the music and harmony is about to occur. As I reported for duty, "Sergeant Andrus come to my office," and I heard "here are your orders. You can start clearing and signing over your equipment tomorrow because you're going to Germany in three months." All of this and I'm only 21 years old.

That night Herv and Dayna were out for the evening. Sparkle and I lay on their living room floor and we talked and shared for hours. We felt like we were in love with each other and I know she had a dramatic effect on me and my feelings, but ultimately, we arrived at this conclusion. I couldn't and wouldn't expect her to wait for me while I was in Germany for 3 ½ years.

I was uncertain about my career in the military and I didn't know where the future for my life would plant its roots. This was another deployment or change in duty station that was going to leave me friendless and lonely. It was awesome to find love that I was committed to and felt great about, but my season hadn't manifested itself yet. The instability caused me to revert back to the whoremonger choices and promiscuous ways. HOW LONG DOES IT TAKE?

Ezekiel 36: 26

A new heart also will I give you, and a new spirit will I put within you: and I will take away the stony heart out of your flesh, and I will give you an heart of flesh.

My vain existence and behavior started to dissipate, but time was still needed to come to the recognition and decimation of the issue. The heart of humankind can be massaged to love by our spiritual relationship, and affiliation with God. His grace and favor annihilates and crucifies our sin, iniquity, and evil doing. Relationships begin at a chance or opportunity and we are best suited to be in a relationship if we know where we are going in life. God is the only focus that tears down the barriers that will surely appear after the so-called commitment in a relationship. Clearly, I wasn't at that moment, so Sparkle didn't have to suffer through the Marvin that Tuckina had suffered from such an early age. Can you see some of the change? Some change doesn't stop bashing and crucifying people's feelings and trust. As long as we vainly live, then so shall we torture the emotions and daily lives of others!

  McCully Barracks in Wackernheim, Germany would be my fifth duty station in 4 ½ years. I had actually requested to be stationed in Germany when I finished my basic training at Ft. Bliss, Texas in 1984, because my brothers Reggie, Roy and my cousin Wade were all in Germany at that time. When I arrived in Germany Roy and Wade were still there, but Roy was six hours away in West Berlin and Wade was three hours away in Stuttgart.

  Traveling back and forth to visit them put me in contact with several different European women. During my three-hour ride from Stuttgart one morning at 2am, I hit black ice on the Autobahn traveling at 195 mph. The car slides out of control to the side of the road but I didn't flip or hit anything. It would appear that warning and destruction couldn't be any clearer with God steppin in. If you can't fathom how fast 195 mph is, then you won't realize that, that was a brush with death.

GOD KNOWS YOUR NAME!

My brother, Roy, was one of the top DJ's in Europe, so being his little brother in a night club paid big promiscuous dividends! I also had a friend in my unit that was on his second tour of duty in Germany. He couldn't wait to take me to Frankfurt, Germany so I could see the Red Light District. In Germany prostitution is legal and it is controlled and monitored by the government.

That wasn't exciting to me, because while I was stationed in Ft. Hood, TX, at the age of 18, I picked up a prostitute in order to quench my curiosity. That was $35 wasted. Questions and curiosities about the darker parts of life and living draw Christians into uncharacteristic territory especially in our impressionable years of life. My departure from the proper raising that my mother enforced was being used for improper purposes.

While I was in Germany, I begin to miss family and family gatherings and the love and peace found in being around them. Often, I would get invited to various functions or parties and I was always the odd one in the bunch, because everyone else was married. That would cause me to think about Sparkle, so what would I do to change those feelings? You know the answer. What I should've done was call or write to her. Being ignorant applies to every portion of our lives. This knowledge should lead us into the search for truth in spirit and emotion.

I played softball at high a level and the team would travel for games all around Germany. I joined the German American Contact Club. We toured all around Germany's Cassels and country side. I traveled to other countries like Spain, Amsterdam, Denmark and some others. The life of a player was good at that time. My awful behavior always squelched and banished my family desires and loneliness for the institution of family that owes itself to the plan of God.

Genesis 1:26-28
26 And God said, Let us make man in our image, after our likeness: and let them have dominion over the fish of the

sea, and over the fowl of the air, and over the cattle, and over all the earth, and over every creeping thing that creepeth upon the earth. ²⁷ So God created man in his own image, in the image of God created he him; male and female created he them. ²⁸ And God blessed them, and God said unto them, Be fruitful, and multiply, and replenish the earth, and subdue it: and have dominion over the fish of the sea, and over the fowl of the air, and over every living thing that moveth upon the earth.

After a day at work, a soldier of mine asked if I could drive him to see his girlfriend. I said sure. When we arrived at the Deli where she was waiting, he asked if I would come in to meet her. As I entered the Deli, I looked behind the counter and I saw this beautiful, light complexioned woman serving customers. My soldier said, Sarg., this is Millie, my girlfriend. Clearly you could see that his girlfriend and the lady serving customers were related. I asked about her and Millie said that's my sister, Nandy.

Nandy and I met and from the first few minutes, her innocent spirit sparked something in me. Her father was Black American and her mother was German and I didn't say she was innocent. I desired family so much and the instability of my military career had me longing for something concrete, so I dated Nandy for a while and asked her to marry me. We went to Denmark and got married. Because I got married and moved to military housing, the Army added an additional year to the length of my tour of duty in Germany. What isn't seen are talked about in this narrative is my love for Sparkle, Sparkle, the beautiful, kind and gentle woman that I left in Seattle.

GOD KNOWS YOUR NAME!

Nandy didn't put any restrictions on me and she let me come and go as I pleased. She failed to hold me accountable. Maybe it was because she was focused on having the baby that she was pregnant with when I met her, so she just didn't see what was really going on with me. The trips to Berlin and Stuttgart never stopped. From Frankfurt to Mannheim and then some, I had sexual affairs and women thinking maybe one day that this good, decent, Christian man would fall in love with them and stay with them.

That's the emotional content and instability that exists when Christians don't lie, but they just live a lie. Nandy's best friend would come over to have dinner with us on several occasions. German customs are simple and they don't leave things undone. Nandy would take the dishes to the kitchen after dinner and she would wash dry and save the dishes before returning to the living room.

One evening I had taken my shower and was lounging in my robe and Nandy was in the kitchen doing the dishes when suddenly her best friend opened my robe and began to perform oral sex on me. True love would've made me stop her, put her out and inform Nandy of the fact that she wasn't her friend, but she was a backstabbing, conniving hoe.

I didn't stop her and to make it worst I lied to Nandy the next morning saying that I was going to work a little earlier, but I went to her best friend's apartment and started a sexual affair that lasted for almost a year, until my conscience caught up with me. That choice would separate me from God for years. Notice I separated from God, God didn't separate His self from me and that's the perfect nature of grace and mercy.

Late one evening leaving the club a young lady asked if we could give her a ride home. Joseph and I said sure. The sex that followed involving the three of us led to a mistake that I'm sorry to think about to this day! Joseph and I fell asleep and when we woke up it was time for us to report for duty. We raced to the barracks with no time to spare before going on our unit run that morning. Nandy knew that I had been unfaithful from that moment and she never trusted me again. I really ripped her heart out and the worst was yet to come, because after my conscience caught up with me, I finally told her about the affair with her best friend, Slaudia.

Hear me and hear me well!!! Nandy told me later that she would have conversations about our sex life with Slaudia. If you ever want to open the door for Satan, let him know where you're the weakest. Even after all the wrong and sin, I still refused to pray for help and forgiveness. χριστιανός warnings before the destruction are nothing new, just as our ignorance and failure to heed them isn't anything new. At this point of my life, despair started to ease its way in. HOW LONG DOES IT TAKE? Yes, the question still remains, and apparently, I was incapable or too immature to answer it.

Chapter 10: Adulterer's Brushes with Death

Sitting at home on a Sunday evening relaxing and watching a little TV, the phone rang. It was the duty Officer from the Unit on Post calling to tell me that I needed to come into the barracks on Post McCully in Wachernheim, Germany. At that time, I had already done everything required for me to leave Germany for my next duty station which was Army Recruiting Command in Newburg, New Jersey. I asked him what was going on and he said that he couldn't say over the phone.

I thought that one of my soldiers must have gotten into some type of trouble. When I arrived at the barracks, I reported to the 1st Sergeant and he took a copy of my orders and tore them up. He said these are your new orders and that I was to go to the motor pool inventory and sign for my equipment and that I was resuming my position as squad leader, because we are going to Iraq for Operation Desert Storm (1991).

The Army added another year to my time in Germany because of the war. We were due to leave for Iraq in a month. My adultery and cheating on

Nandy was still fresh and demoralizing to her, so I didn't get a, "I could be killed in combat" send off. What a turn of events! Cancel Newburg, New Jersey enter Iraq and some clown name Saddam Hussein. If evil were ever to be found in a man's heart, you could give him credit along with those that stewed up and concocted the Weapons of Mass Destruction deceit and lie to the world. That single three initial, WMD, drumming and drumming from the mouths of liars led close to two million un-knowing soldiers with the bombardment of millions of dollars and pounds of weaponry unleashed on the Iraqi People.

While sitting on the tarmac at King Faud Airport in Saudi Arabia, the New Year 1991 came in and it found me cold, scared and lonely. I refused to let my soldiers and command see the true me. For them, I had to remain a leader that exuded confidence, diligence and courage. They had put our cold weather gear on the wrong transport plane, so we sat for hours without jackets. On that morning, I learned that 50 degrees in the desert is much colder than 35 degrees in Germany.

At that time in the midst of my confidence, diligence and courage, nothing that I was faced with could or would bring me to a breaking point. Once there for some time, I realized that I had been trained and prepared for this moment, this war, and that I had trained and prepared my soldiers as well, however; the decisions and conversations of those leading us caused me great concern. My confidence, diligence and courage indirectly opposed and offended our leadership. From this point and time things, not life, turn for the worst.

My plight had never been considered. I had been militarily bent and shaped for someone's purposes and motives. To lose sight of that would come with a heavy cost. Situations dictate that our visceral awareness and practical awareness stay at the ready. Plight being disregarded, I nakedly walked into a den of plotters and haters with the incorrect rhetoric and tone. Just stay with me and you'll get to know the plotters and haters in the den.

Most of the time, our intuitions, lessons, and experiences guide us accurately when we lean and depend on them. The Holy Spirit must be the head controlling our visceral and practical awareness. We need protection from the situations and issues in life that our instincts and experiences haven't the ability to defeat or overcome. Praying for this monumental position in life is crucial to our spiritual and worldly plight.

GOD KNOWS YOUR NAME!

Do you remember that I was cold, scared and lonely? Well the other planes arrived and brought with them our cold weather gear. I had managed to realize my preparation and training for such a war, but there wasn't anything that I could do to relieve or take away the loneliness that I was feeling. I left Germany as an adulterer and cheating husband of a beautiful, kind, loving and caring wife. When we were allowed to make our first phone calls home, to Germany, I was reminded of that fact. Nandy sounded so bitter and angry toward me that it hit me harder emotionally than any grenade or bullet could have hit me.

I took that loneliness and my strengths as a soldier to a meeting with my supervisors and butted heads with their anger and frustrations with me. I and my brothers are men that were raised to look you in the eye and tell it like it is, but that's not the delivery system that we, humans, appreciate or accept. Emphatically armed with my strengths and infected with their frustrations and anger, the construction, or more accurately spoken the deconstruction, of my plight is set to begin.

At age 25, facing Saddam and his 1.3 million-person military machine couldn't get me to pray. To tell you the truth, I went into Desert Storm unarmed. Living a life without prayer, is living unarmed! But what about all that Christian upbringing, you might ask? I would dare to say that I'm not unique in the realm of a **CHRISTIAN LIVING A LIE**. In the moments before our departure tensions and emotions were off the charts. Now more than ever, the man next to you needed to know that you had your stuff wired tight and that it was together. Our platoon wasn't very close in my opinion and I could have changed that by bringing us together in prayer.

Without boring the masses, I'll say this. My issues with us not being close and faulting the leaders for it became my nemesis. One meeting in Iraq led to an emotionally charged dismissal of everyone and a summons to another meeting that led to me being relieved of duty and charged with communicating a threat to an officer. **Nobody wins in a war and war changes a person.** Guidance and choice were crippling me and I failed to realize it.

We arrived in Saudi Arabia weeks before our equipment and armor. They made us sleep at the port under a shed without walls for a few weeks before they moved us to the Khobar Towers. While waiting there for our equipment to arrive, I was introduced to a young lady that I had risky unprotected sex with on a few occasions. The scud attacks, hurriedly putting on our chemical suits and gas mask, waiting for 20 to 30 minutes for the all-clear alarm, the alarm sounding and the sound of the explosion of the sound barrier multiple times with our Patriot Missiles launching with metal fragments hitting the buildings during the evening made me feel helpless, so I figured why not. I pray that you got all of that because it gives you all of the stupid and ignorant reasons that we abandon God and logic. Ain't that what we Christians do?

I had just left a wife, that didn't say goodbye, in a living hell and I still had the mindset of what she doesn't know, won't hurt her. Please, please, recognize the absence of foundation, stability and responsibility in all of this. When you meet someone that is inconsistent, lies, hits you, calls you names or abuses you, you can expect what to deal with or choose not to enter a relationship with that person, but what do you do when you meet a Christian like myself? Effervescent and Charismatic.

The Christian that didn't treat you with the ugliness mentioned above, but dampened your spirit over time by being uncommitted, polite in saying no, pulled and pushed your chair, honestly said when and where he would be, and lavished you with kindness. That type of Christian is dangerous and lethal, because they are straddling the good and bad fence with a no limit attack on the unsuspected. Be aware people the danger lurks closer than you think. Well let's venture back to Saudi Arabia.

    Shortly after leaving the Khobar Towers, the warhead from a Scud Missile fired by the Iraqis slammed into one of the buildings in the Towers killing several soldiers. For some reason I wanted to say thank God for us not being there for that attack, but I chose to just want to move forward and illuminate the threat. That is failure at the spiritual and moral level. When killing or harming others for another man's cause is your purpose, then you've become an instrument. Not of change or compassion, but of danger and dominance. Tensions were getting higher amongst the soldiers in our unit as we relocated to a location in the desert.

    You can chalk it up to fear of the unknown or just fear itself, but we were a divided unit before we left Germany and a combat situation didn't seem to draw us closer or make us as cohesive as we should have been to start. This was a time when I truly needed Jesus and His wondrous working power! It was a really crazy time. Some soldiers were receiving videos from their wives having sex with other men or multiple men telling them don't worry about coming home I'm being well taken care of. Others were causing self-inflicted wounds by shooting themselves to get sent back to Germany. That caused our commander to face tough scrutiny from our higher command. From all indications, only a small portion of our unit was supposed to be in Iraq, but our commander, said one go we all go.

The stage is set for my personal rage that just needed something to be said or to be asked to set off a major life changing moment! This literary adventure is not just about my being a hot mess or some sex crazed idiot. It contains valuable information that can change and enhance lives just as the wisdom, knowledge and warnings from my grandmother, Clemonce, would do for me. Associated with the wartime topic years prior, she said, "son listen, there are going to be times and people over your life and there is nothing that you can do about it."

When my personal rage over having our ammunition taken from us in a combat zone, the commander talking about training in a combat zone, having to do guard duty without any ammo, bickering and backbiting in our platoon, our lieutenant talking to and asking other units and leaders about us and finally my lieutenant talking to one of my soldiers without my knowledge, which breaks the chain of command, the situation got messy and things came to a boiling point.

At a platoon and squad leaders meeting one evening, I asked the lieutenant a question that wasn't answered to any idiot's satisfaction and the lieutenant got upset with my persistence. I also confronted him about talking to one my soldiers and breaking the chain of command. That led him to say, "the last time I checked I'm the fucking lieutenant and I'm running this fucking platoon." My response to that was, "okay Sir, the next time that my soldiers need toilet paper to wipe their ass, I'll send them to you." He became infuriated and put everyone out of the tent and the sergeants and squad leaders all found humor in my impulsive decision. When those that function under the auspices of Satan and wrong others, that doesn't give the χριστιανός, who is right, the authority to respond or retaliate in the wrong manner.

We really have to pause for a moment in all we do when it's possible. That moment may allow time for our visceral, spiritual and intellectual wisdom to shape our decisions and choices in our course of necessary actions. Actions in response, rhetoric and tone, to the wrong may not be warranted at all, especially if The Holy Spirited says "I got this". Nobody wins in a war and war changes a person. I can still hear those explosions and the metal fragments the artillery hitting the side of the building that we were confined to because of faulty planning and arrogance!

At this point according to my cousin, Clarence Dunbar Sr, I was the dumbest person in the world, because I thought I knew everything. If we know everything, then what is there left for God to work with? The next morning, I was summons to a meeting with my lieutenant and platoon sergeant and I didn't see it coming. I walked out of that tent relieved of duty and placed under armed guard. My spirit started to feel as if this was the punishment or rebuke from the Lord for my faults and failure as a husband and a χριστιανός.

My military plight had been altered and corrupted. Up until that moment, I was one of the best protectors of democracy that the United States Army had to offer. I failed to heed the words of wisdom from my grandmother and life became increasingly unbalanced. My statement of fact is *nobody wins in a war and war changes a man.* That cannot be stated enough or overstated. When I look back, I see the approach Satan used, and it was a chump and a weasel. Lord, I fell for it and landed hard and the worse for it. It was a "do you wanna be right" or "be a career soldier" moment, and being right was the focus.

Just a few words of wisdom from past experience and intellectual discovery, my family from the Broussard side of things has always been straight forward in our conversation and opinions. We don't talk about you behind your back with sneaky rhetoric and tone. Since we abide in a world that thrives on that sneaky talk, we've had to bear the burden and wrath of those that operate with the "who do you think you are" perspective in their supervisory roles.

For this reason, I need to caution you first to consider your plight accompanied with prayer for humility and safe passage. Be aware that if you strike Satan, absent of The Holy Spirit, Satan will hit back. Our rhetoric and tone if armed and shrouded in faith and righteousness will not seem to impact the worldly conscious folk, but it'll be much better for us and our reward in the fulness of time. Failure to follow instructions cripples χριστιανός and hinders our superiority over evil. Stay prayerful, faithful and grateful in all that you do and speak.

I SAID IN THE BEGINNING THAT I DIDN'T WANT TO MARGINALIZE OR DIMINISH THE IMPACT OR EFFECTIVENESS OF THE INFORMATION, FACTS, AND THE STORY. I'M ALSO NOT TRYING TO REWRITE THE BIBLE. FOR THOSE REASONS, YOU HAVEN'T SEEN THE INJECTION OF SCRIPTURE FOR A FEW PARAGRAPHS, BUT LET'S BE CLEAR. THIS HAS EVERYTHING TO DO WITH THE WORD OF GOD!!!

GOD KNOWS YOUR NAME!

Chapter 11: Recklessness or Malfeasance

The Word of God says that you can't kick against the pricks. I want to add the establishment to that. The wisdom and visceral fabric of our being should guide us in these moments of conflict and frustration in dealing with Christians and the establishment or government. Against all visceral warnings, I kicked which led in essence to me squandering all that I had worked for. We have to be far more careful not to kick against the Word of God or fail to adhere to the Word of God. I had a failure to follow instructions and I kicked.

Acts 9:4-6

4 And he fell to the earth, and heard a voice saying unto him, **Saul, Saul, why persecutest thou me?** **5** And he said, Who art thou, Lord? And the Lord said, **I am Jesus whom thou persecutest: it is hard for thee to kick against the pricks.** **6** And he trembling and astonished said, Lord, what wilt thou have me to do? And the Lord said unto him, **Arise, and go into the city, and it shall be told thee what thou must do.**

We inadvertently come across those that seek our failure or demise as we proceed with intentions to overcome difficulties, distractions, hindrances and pestilences for the fruition of our path as children of God. We as χριστιανός are consecrated to function and operate on a higher plane. In this realm, the fruition of us navigating the mandate to honor and obey The Holy Spirit and the establishment is attainable and achievable.

The following scriptures will help you to associate with and understand the establishment. Be mindful of the tricks and snares of the establishment, this is what they tried with Jesus. God wants us to be still and silent as He handles, changes, and fixes the heart and spirit of our enemies.

Matthew 22:15-21

[15] Then went the Pharisees, and took counsel how they might entangle him in his talk. [16] And they sent out unto him their disciples with the Herodians, saying, Master, we know that thou art true, and teachest the way of God in truth, neither carest thou for any man: for thou regardest not the person of men. [17] Tell us therefore, What thinkest thou? Is it lawful to give tribute unto Caesar, or not? [18] But Jesus perceived their wickedness, and said, **Why**

tempt ye me, ye hypocrites? [19] **Shew me the tribute money.** And they brought unto him a penny. [20] And he saith unto them, **Whose is this image and superscription?** [21] They say unto him, Caesar's. Then saith he unto them, **Render therefore unto Caesar the things which are Caesar's; and unto God the things that are God's.**

Death and destruction of humans, animals, and infrastructures all around haunts and terrorizes you daily if not constantly. I had an Article 15 hearing in the Army for an issue with my lieutenant, I informed the commander of a great deal of wrong doing by my superiors and it didn't go well for them either. I made the decision to leave the military that day and I still had to return to Germany and the family mess that I had left behind. I made the wrong choice. I chose to be combative and standoffish when I should've retreated and prayed for the situation and possible outcomes to be made clearer for all of us. When calamity is all around, be heavenly focused and continue to control your senses while considering your plight and the position of others.

PTSD, chemical exposure, depression, rashes, chronic pain, sleep apnea and gulf war syndrome is what I and several hundreds of thousands of soldiers brought back from Iraq. Nobody wins in a war and war changes a person. Now, back in Germany I have to deal with the pain and agony that I put my wife through before I left for Desert Storm, so it was time for the talk. I started with I'm sorry for my actions and infidelity. She responded with I slept with two soldiers on multiple occasions while you were gone. I paused for a minute or two and then I replied "okay I deserved that." Keep your head up χριστιανός and be confident in your superiority over evil.

GOD KNOWS YOUR NAME!

Hebrews 13:3-5

³ Remember them that are in bonds, as bound with them; and them which suffer adversity, as being yourselves also in the body. ⁴ Marriage is honourable in all, and the bed undefiled: but whoremongers and adulterers God will judge. ⁵ Let your conversation be without covetousness; and be content with such things as ye have: for he hath said, I will never leave thee, nor forsake thee.

We made love that evening and I thought that our marriage was going to survive and began to repair itself, because I was ready to be the χριστιανός husband that I was supposed to be, but wait a minute. I had slaughtered and killed all of Nandy's trust in me. Over the next 3 years, I diligently lived for showing Nandy that she could trust me and that I loved only her, but that was a fleeting attempt.

In her mind, if I left the apartment I was leaving to go and cheat, or be with her best friend, Slaudia. That is what my faults as a Christian, a man, and a husband had accomplished. I really toed the line in the following few months and didn't have much time remaining on my enlistment in the Army. With time whining down on my tour of duty in Germany, I asked Nandy if she would be coming to the United States with me when I exited the Army and she said no. To make some extra money in preparation for that time, I began moonlighting at a Mexican restaurant called Chi-Chi's located in the military housing complex where we lived.

I really tried hard with all of my fiber and being to show Nandy how seriously and sincerely sorry I was about my infidelity and actions with other women and her best friend and that I would be the husband that she thought she was marrying. Life for me was cold and desolate and there was a much more vicious attack happening beyond my knowledge. An attack aimed at the slow and total destruction of a person. Do you remember **no one wins in a war and war changes a man?** Keep that in mind.

At my moonlighting job I started as a waiter and later became a bartender. That's just what we Christians do. The recklessness of a husband and the malfeasance of a χριστιανός is what you should be seeing. I made the bulk of my money from tips. Being a waiter / bartender came easy to me and I was great at it. There isn't much good in handling and serving alcohol, however; I did make over $3,500.00 in preparation for my exit from the Army. Later I loaned all of that money and a couple of hundred more dollars to my closest brother. I worked with some pretty awesome people at Chi-Chi's! I can't remember a single time or event that involved someone's selfish act or ambition. The teamwork was off the chain from supervisor to hosts and hostesses.

Where is the presence of this nature in the church? Love and socialism in a substantive form in the church is so pleasing to God. The church is a people that are struggling to understand where they stop and God starts. The state of the church is suffering from the cohesive deficiency spurned by the intolerable need to be us. The Christian and their greed along with their Christian personality has damaged the credibility of God among the sinful sick. That's only two descriptions of such behavior from Christians.

I took another 6 hour ride to West Berlin to visit my brother, Roy, one last time before my return to the United States. It was time for me to leave and everything went well with the visit, until I got in the car and realized that I had forgotten my glasses. I had to go back into the studio and I found him heating up a spoon with a syringe on the table. He was preparing to get high. At the time that I found him doing drugs, our oldest brother was in prison dying from drug complications and AIDS, and our brother next to him had committed suicide from his drug addiction. It hurt me to see what drugs were doing to my brothers and the emotional torture that my mother was going through with each incident or situation that involved her children.

Later, I helped relocate my brother from Germany to Seattle, Washington with me and I tried to love him past his drug addiction, but his next high was all he was concerned about. He died some years later from a heart condition in my mother's house in Opelousas, Louisiana while she was in another room.

She found his lifeless body and called me. There was a crack pipe lying on the floor next to his foot. *3 out of 5 children dead for a mother who still has decades to live, how much more can this woman of God bear?*

    I hid my despair from Nandy, soldiers, friends and peers. While hiding my despair, I continued to add to it with my behavior. I had a certain flair and charm that attracted married women in Chi-Chi's. I listened attentively and let everything be about them and that's all they really wanted. To be thousands of miles away from home and to feel like you've lost your husband to a video game was a promiscuity windfall for a predator or should I say Christian like myself. Hurting and lying to Nandy wasn't as horrible as the lie I was living!!! I possessed one year to be complicit in adultery on almost a nightly basis. Our adulterous thoughts generally lead to poor choices. From 9 years of age to 25 years of age indulgent in sin, and God still hadn't removed his hand from me or my soul. I tried to mask my despair with vain and beguiled actions.

    To this dead end, I know this; The thoughts, conversations, and actions of men and women offer explicit and implicit realities that fracture the being, fabric, and fiber of humanity's most precious resources, LOVE and TRUST. We must examine and explore the recesses in our existence both spiritual and physical to eliminate recklessness and malfeasance as the living breath of God. We being the living breath of God, must fill and develop our recesses to a maturity that embarks on a spiritual foundation. Pay attention to the word **offer** mentioned above. You can accept or reject an offer.

GOD KNOWS YOUR NAME!

Chapter 12: The Repetition of a Husband

I decided that I wanted to live in Seattle, Washington after my departure from the Army. I left Germany and my wife, Nandy, didn't leave with me. My friend Herv and I kept in contact with each other over the years. He said that I could stay with them, and use their third car until I got settled and financially situated.

Later I would dramatically learn that, that time frame was one week. After years of silence and distance from Herv, he finally said that the reason he put me out of his home was because I had loaned the $3,500.00 to my brother. His relationship with his family was different from mine with my family and he didn't understand the out-pouring of love or the gesture. Remember he was showing me love by allowing me to live there and use their vehicle. **Go figure?????** He tried over the years to earn my forgiveness and he did, but our friendship was dissolved. Who gets bit twice by the same snake?

With less than $100.00, I went to an apartment complex a couple of blocks away from

Herv's home and I was able to rent an apartment with no deposit or furniture. I had to rent transportation until my car arrived from Germany. I was in a really dark place in life and I wanted to give up. My state of mind was leading me to believe that whatever I touched or cared about I made it toxic from relationships to daily common living. I didn't pray but I just hung in there and circumstances started to change. I know now not by my strength or might, but only that of The Father which is in Heaven.

Zechariah 4:6
Then he answered and spake unto me, saying, This is the word of the Lord unto Zerubbabel, saying, Not by might, nor by power, but by my spirit, saith the Lord of hosts.

I began to have work from labor ready every day. I found permanent employment as a cashier / clerk at an ARCO gas station and with Burns Security. That led to employment with the Postal Service and ultimately as a Corrections Officer with King County Dept of Adult Detention. I wasn't praying for myself, but somebody was and did. This isn't a soap opera, but if you wanted a good one this would be the one you should start with.

Working almost day and night for months began to payoff. I had a bank account, furniture, my car from Germany and I even step foot in a church. Making it and constantly working wiped away despair, so I thought. Stacking paper didn't remove the sting that I felt about my marital situation. I kept constant communication with Nandy trying to ensure and guarantee her that I know I made a huge mistake. I was truly and was extremely sorry. I expressed my love and desire for her to be in Seattle with me.

Seven months had passed since I left Germany and I hadn't taken any time off from work or had any leisure time since I arrived in Washington. I decided to catch a movie at the theatre. A truck driver from Sioux Falls, South Dakota opened the door at the theatre and that's how I got to know that she was from Sioux Falls. Seven months of faithfulness, a major and life changing accomplishment, blaspheme that probably astonished Satan himself. Sioux Falls opened a door that stayed open and it opened every time her route bought her to Washington.

The next day, I met a young lady while I was doing some training for the postal service. We began to talk on the phone casually for a month and suddenly she said, come see me. The choice and decision that I made on that evening complicated, distorted and vandalized my life and those that cared most about me. Without making excuses, I've fallen and resumed my **CHRISTIAN LIVING LIE** in full effect. The girlfriend that I mentioned above became pregnant and pregnant again and I urged her to abort the second child. I sighted all of my thoughts and circumstances as the reason why this birth shouldn't happen. I basically forced her into an impulsive decision in an attempt to appease me and my dead spirit. Baby Mama now.

I struggled for years with trying to find a way to forgive myself for that decision and the burden that I placed on her. She was more devastated than I had ever made anyone in this **CHRISTIAN LIVING LIE** of mine!!! Whenever we would speak with each other it was clearly and spiritually evident that she felt like I made a murderer out of her. I remained as is during this. Just as vain and aimless as I wanted to be. You won't be able to grasp the full extent of what I'm writing until it comes to your front door, or more correct, your back door. Notice that I'm accepting all of the burden of our actions. I'm accepting it because God requires χριστιανός men to lead us in the faith of holiness and righteousness.

GOD KNOWS YOUR NAME!

Genesis 2:15-17

15 And the Lord God took the man, and put him into the garden of Eden to dress it and to keep it. 16 And the Lord God commanded the man, saying, Of every tree of the garden thou mayest freely eat: 17 But of the tree of the knowledge of good and evil, thou shalt not eat of it: for in the day that thou eatest thereof thou shalt surely die.

I had to let my wife know about Marvin Jr, but I kept the second pregnancy and abortion from her. Then, caught completely off guard and astonished to be honest, Nandy decided to join me and my issues in Seattle. By that time, I had purchased my first new home and had a well-paying job as a correction officer. Sioux Falls, Malaysia and Baby Mama had already put shoes under the bed when Nandy made the decision to join me. I asked a God loving, true friend, Valerie, to help with establishing Nandy in her new home and surroundings, however; trusting me was unattainable. She just couldn't handle the possible subjection to that pain and demeaning again.

Thank you, Valerie, for all that you did in making the transition for Nandy go as smooth as possible and the encouragement and prayers that you offered and prayed for us. I had a huge amount of baggage that came with me, Baby Mama drama. It was a mountain of emotional content far too much for her to handle. We divorced and she returned to Germany. Thirty years old and so many people have been corrupted or entangled with my deviant and menacing behavior. All this time had passed and Tuckina from Opelousas was still holding on. From Opelousas, across Texas, to Korea, from Washington, to Germany and back to Washington with a few more chapters to write. The **CHRISTIAN LIVING LIE** will come true.

After the divorce, I pondered on what happened in that situation, and questions developed in my thoughts. Did Nandy decide to come to Washington just to see or visit the United States? No, that wasn't it, because we came home for my grandmother's funeral. Did she want to see the new house and cars that she would live in and drive? What she really didn't expect was my oldest son's mother showing up in a see through, laced night gown with flesh being the most visible in the picture. Whatever the reason be it love or another chance, she couldn't get back to Germany fast enough. I didn't stop my Christian behavior as a husband or a father. Malaysia was just introduced in the previous paragraph. I snuck that one in, and you may or may not learn more about that **CHRISTIAN LIVING LIE** because of her, well that just was for me to break.

We unwillingly drag people and their spirits through a living hell with our mess and foolishness. We live in absence of thought or care for what our transgressions may bring upon those who are innocently praying and hoping to be cared for and loved. This life, that is inherently a crucial part of us, speaks to a life that is without guidance and proper choices. If I had acted on some of my indulgent propensity, I would've lived in Sioux Falls, Sweden, Malaysia, Montana or Berlin and a few that aren't worth mentioning. How awful can the men of this world be that women would settle for a man that is non-committal or even non-caring to be factual?

In all of these offers, I didn't have to work, provide, love or commit to anything concrete. My mild manners and indulgence were the assumption of a future and these women allowed me to steal their character and virtue. This situation is possible because we let our emotions and actions take us from 0 - 60 faster than we can spell comprehension. This is also where the tendencies for making impulsive decisions are stored. With this fallacy, Satan's deception, the Holy Spirit isn't consulted and therefore; unheard. This is what Marvin Jr. was born into and it started to show in the early years of his life just as it did for me not having my deceased father around.

Ruth 3:9-12

⁹ And he said, Who art thou? And she answered, I am Ruth thine handmaid: spread therefore thy skirt over thine handmaid; for thou art a near kinsman. ¹⁰ And he said, Blessed be thou of the Lord, my daughter: for thou hast shewed more kindness in the latter end than at the beginning, inasmuch as thou followedst not young men, whether poor or rich. ¹¹ And now, my daughter, fear not; I will do to thee all that thou requirest: for all the city of my people doth know that thou art a virtuous woman. ¹² And now it is true that I am thy near kinsman: howbeit there is a kinsman nearer than I.

Chapter 13: Behavior With a Digging Shovel

After my debacle as a husband, life took "an as a matter-of-fact direction" meaning, I lived by what was fact. Failed as a husband, fostered a child out of wedlock, no prayer life or church affiliation, frequenting night clubs, sleeping around with this one and that one, letting sex determine my direction and course of action, deteriorating physical condition, no care or concerns about much, over working under achieving, digging deeper holes of despair, no guidance poor choices and no God fearing attitude.

What can come of such actions in life? No one wins in a war, and war changes a man is playing a major role in all of this, but not to my knowledge, nor the knowledge of those that are in my path. It was clear to see if you noticed the countless hours of work that I had been doing over the past few years. Dark days of depression were masked with working helloes and smiles. At some points, eating a bullet became a real option for me. It became common place as if it was a walk in the park. As you can see, I'm still here, God steps in with the truth. I am His. Let's continue to discuss the other options.

Now I'm a dad at age 29 and really don't know how to take care of myself much less a baby. Life centered on me and not consideration, responsibility, obligation, trespassing or repercussion. I did do the right thing financially concerning him according to the courts. Working and sexing was a day for me to include sleeping with a 63-year-old woman that lived in the same apartment complex as I. She just oozed with confidence. What could I say to approach her at her level of distinction? That was her attitude in our first conversation.

I had learned how to play chess while I was in Iraq. Believe it or not a black brotha from Connecticut named Jackson taught me in between scud attacks while at the Khobar Towers in Saudi Arabia. Thanks Jack you were what I needed my brotha. I would play chess with some of the inmates at the jail sometimes. I did it to develop a more personal relationship with them to see if I could get more cooperation and less death threats. They needed to know that I was more than just a uniform and a badge. Fresh out of the military, I was a champion for the rules and control measures. Later in my travels, I learned how to play golf, so you can see a shift in life is occurring.

There was a decline in the guidance and choice issues that I had been facing for the past twenty years. It's amazing what playing chess and playing golf can do. We have the propensity to live demoralizing and depressing lives, but if we can grasp a hold of the simple things formulated by a prayer life, and abandon impulsive decision making we can alter our course of sin and shine in our Father's, God, marvelous light. For the better part of my adolescent ages, I indulged and wallowed in my propensity to chase after the good women to tarnish mainly the type and stature of women that I described earlier. The mistake that we make is assuming that humankind always does that on purpose. For me, it was a preference and not a conscience effort. However, two or three women of any type or stature would always accept my presence and call for sex at any time.

Indulgence still felt great to me and the debauchery would continue as I lived in the absence of the church and prayer. I'm almost certain, that those that were complicit in my indulgence and debauchery lived in the absence of the church and prayer as well. This posture ushered in a relationship with an older white woman that I began a sexual relationship with while her husband lay in their home dying of cancer. Caught and arrested for soliciting prostitutes caused him to ignore her. He hadn't touched her in years.

GOD KNOWS YOUR NAME!

Enter Marvin ready, willing and able to do his duty with all of the trimmings of his Christian upbringing, nice manners, inviting attitude and savior of the day mentality. I relentlessly pursued her from the moment I saw her coming into work. As a central control officer in the jail, I made sure every door and elevator were ready for her movements and responsibilities in the building. Daily I greeted her as if I hadn't seen her in years and I smiled at her with the cunning of a gator moving in on an unknowing baby deer at a watering hole. She too had the strong will, character, and personality. See the pattern, and know that she was in the beginning stages of a hurt and torment non-committal journey that involved her feelings and actions for me.

<u>*Don't misunderstand this, she wasn't a target or a victim nor was she a character in a scheme to be the subject in a book.*</u> She suited my promiscuous preference and I just had to have her. I had her sexually and she had me. Somewhere in our affair, she desired more of me and I desired more of her and other women as well. I was later sued by that same woman for having a meretricious relationship with her. The lawsuit was based on the premise that I had made implicit and explicit long term relational and financial promises to her that I defaulted on.

I never lied to women and I never made promises. I just treated them nice and great on some occasions without emotional attachment, that **CHRISTIAN LIVING LIE**. After several attorney meetings, legal wrangling, legal fees and a deposition, I decided to settle the case for about $35,000.^{00} if memory serves me accurately. I settled the lawsuit to stop the pillaging and pilfering of my hard work and finances which were being decimated by folks in the legal profession.

At the deposition, I learned and witnessed how much pain and agony that I had caused that woman without malice or intent. I'm only responsible for what I do, and cause was a gigantic statement that weighed in dramatically at the outset. Promiscuity and preference made me a predator and it came with a heavy price for hurting someone with my Godless living. Sure, I paid a price, but I have yet to pay the full cost for my actions. This isn't a guilty plea because my intent was neutral, but what does neutrality look like for a Christian. I know that my vain life, and living was the measure for strong, positive women to fail from their direction of achievement and success. Maybe getting involved with me didn't cripple them, but it didn't benefit them in the long run. Never find yourself subservient to someone that is without distinct motive or clear directives.

Earlier, I claimed to have stopped stealing. That wasn't accurate. I wasn't lying or misleading anyone, but the truth is I was still stealing, because I used honesty, candor and my sly smile to engage in actions that prompted an emotional response and acceptance of my propensity to stone wall. Direct or indirect is the same as tomato or tumatto. Deception in any form is seen as deception in the eyes of the Lord. I'm blessed with the Lord's forgiveness and I have been given the forgiveness I sought from those in the wake of my vain **CHRISTIAN LIVING LIE**. If we desire to be made whole again, then we must allow the necessary changes to occur in our hearts and minds. God is after the heart of man, so clean it up, lift Him up, and stop stealing.

GOD KNOWS YOUR NAME!

John 5:8-9,14,15

[8] Jesus saith unto him, **Rise, take up thy bed, and walk.** [9] And immediately the man was made whole, and took up his bed, and walked: and on the same day was the sabbath.

[14] Afterward Jesus findeth him in the temple, and said unto him, **Behold, thou art made whole: sin no more, lest a worse thing come unto thee.** [15] The man departed, and told the Jews that it was Jesus, which had made him whole.

From the heavenly position that your heart takes as it concerns God, He can start building bridges for your safe passage from **then and there to here and now**. The fruition of God's injected valor definitely removes the sting of what we have directly or indirectly imposed upon one another.

I made another attempt at being a husband. I went against the odds and married a co-worker. We snuck off to Las Vegas and got married the next day. We had a short honeymoon at Lake Tahoe. A pattern and pair of next day marriages that failed is starring us in the face. I married solely on the fact that we had agreed that the two of us could have a good life together. That was based upon the following perks of our status, meaning good jobs, middle class, similar level of love and care for each other, desire to own stuff and the possibility of financial freedom down the line. However, at this point I had been promiscuous and attempted to have sexual affairs with more of the female officers than I can remember. The nature of their hiring was the confidence and strength in their existence. So quite naturally, they should be aware of me.

  The ever presence of other women that I frolicked around with continued to plagued any serious relationship that I had. I lied to both of my wives to be with several different women and let me remind you that these women all wanted my commitment to loving them on a permanent basis. At this very moment, graves of sin and immorality are being prepared and retro-fitted for my assault on the unknowing and their families, yes, there families. Relatives, children, friends, and co-workers all get to experience, see, and testify to your **CHRISTIAN LIVING LIE**, deep southern charm, effervescence, and well-groomed manners.

It may sound as if I just sought after sex with different women all day and every day that I was living. <u>NOT SO</u>. I had hobbies, work, children and friends with my vain existence and absence of spiritual goals. What I really needed was the church and The Holy Spirit. **Again, don't let the sex narrative block the impact of the absence of prayer and commitment narrative.** The framework of the book is all inclusive, so my faults as a father, husband, person and Christian are all in the narrative. All of the above were in the structure of my life, and they were hampered and scarred by my vain existence. Changes needed to be made and prayer had better come soon.

I was the good Christian with propensity, patience, persistence, time and nothing to lose. That's who we truly are when we're heartless. I acted like a chameleon and turned my life into a promiscuity playground without any amount of intellectual focus or conscience effort. I'm not convinced that people are that naïve to consort with me in that manner, but propensity to feed the flesh is overwhelming. Without God, there is no heart and without heart there is no love. My second wife was willing to live with that and she was confident that that was in my past and honestly it was.

In my view, I could see the family and the house on the corner with the little white picket fence that I desired long ago. We attended church at St John a couple of times and things seemed to be heading in a Christian direction for us. I was faithful and committed in this marriage and I felt great about our decision to marry each other, but the devil was lurking in the wings. Since we had married on a worldly foundation, we didn't seek spiritual assistance in our marital test and trials. That left the front and back door open for the haters and snakes. Don't discuss your bedroom with other people.

Women that I had affairs with and the women who turned me down along with the male officers began to talk and spread rumors and some facts about my sexual behavior. They knew just who to talk with to keep the conversation going and it would eventually reach my wife who was at home on maternity leave. The daily and constant barrage of lies and past history weighed heavily on her especially with the physical and mental challenges that she was bearing during pregnancy. After the birth of our son, my second son, we couldn't survive the devil's attacks on our marriage. Compassion and sympathy weren't what I possessed and was prepared to give. Who do we run to and where must we cry? It's pivotal to know the answer to the questions.

Early one morning after my graveyard shift at the jail, I went to my home to pick up my son for some father son time. Another man answered the door, my door. My second wife and I were separated, so that wasn't the issue. It was the attitude that he had in my house answering my door sucking his teeth with his chest all puffed up. He said that she had already taken our son to daycare and that they weren't home. He almost died that day. I literally placed my hand on my service weapon and sized him up for two to the chest and one to the head. That was my emotions going from 0 - 60 in seconds. God's intervention is mysterious in more ways than we can imagine.

Divorce number two brought with it more issues and drama. My hands and actions remained on the shovel that dug more and more into ugliness. The second marriage didn't have room or plans to exist with my first son. She hated the thought of Marvin Jr.'s mother and family. She used every ounce of her dissatisfaction to steer me away from them. The relationship or paternal obligation shared with the baby mama drama that I created with a one-night stand during my first marriage was unbearable.

GOD KNOWS YOUR NAME!

Marvin Jr.'s mother came to our home early one morning unannounced after I returned home from work. The wife worked the morning shift and I worked the graveyard shift. We had sex in the empty upstairs bedroom. When she left, she immediately got on the car phone and called wife number two and told her this, "I just left your house, Marvin and I fucked the shit out of each other in your bedroom." The wife came home while I was mowing the lawn. She called me a, "mother fucking cheating bastard," and threw her wedding and engagement rings at me to never be found. The middle class living and financial freedom desires and plans are shot. Property, homes, cash and children had to be mitigated and dealing with the pain and stress hadn't started yet.

During this time frame, I stupidly lost a couple of years of time with my first son, Marvin Jr. The children always suffer from crappy and irresponsible decisions made by Christian parents. The question how long does it take still remains being a focal point in my life. Unwillingly knowing of the damage created in my wake, I continued to live recklessly and destructively on what is becoming a hostile level and the battle would be waged in the courts. I would incur child support and bills on a massive scale and working more overtime at the place of employment that was the catalyst for my current situation, was my only way of escape. "When we commit to become, we must sacrifice to the level of our commitment." "If we vow to be a Christian, then we must change to be a χριστιανός," and sacrifice our flesh and spirits through loving God, Jesus and the Holy Spirit in obedience to, of, and in His word. Not so for me just yet, the waters are still too murky and my Christian atrocities have yet to reach their peak.

Chapter 14: The Picture Gets Clearer

Reaching out to my oldest son, Marvin Jr. became one of my priorities in addition to stabilizing my financial situation. God and the church were still on hold. Earlier I had received information from my oldest son's mother that she was pregnant with another child for me. I did everything in my speech and power to get her to abort that child. What kind of monster have I become is what I was thinking after trying to console her one day after the abortion. In all of this we must recognize the complicit actions of all parties and participants no matter the avenue or approach of the bidder or biddee! Let's get back to the monster. Remember, I wasn't dark hearted.

I've been called a lot of things being a combat veteran and corrections officer, but to call myself a monster elevated the height of my Christian atrocities. I felt as thou someone had ripped my insides out and shown them to me! Once certain acts have been committed, we can't undo them and forgiveness for those acts would be far off in the distance loaded and ready to resurface, remind, reclaim and reverberate. In these times we must be able to tap into a much higher level in our relationship with God, because the claim, guilt, and thoughts of being a monster led to perishable actions and further atrocities.

As I lay in the bed of an older woman, who was as complicit in our sexual relationship as I was, she said, "Marvin you're nothing but a nice dog." That wasn't my moniker, but it was accurate and true. After she said that, I began to think back over my years and my daddy came to mind. I never revealed the level of distain and depressive thoughts that she had sparked from that comment. I was weak and powerless to change anything in my life and cared for nothing more than a mediocre existence.

So many of us attach our lives to that type of individual or person, and we do it without recognizing the foothold or impact that it had on the circumference of our lives, the ones we love, and the incoming situations of life. There is no strength, no direction, no future, and no God in a whoremonger moniker. The truth has been told and I still made those visits to my father's grave but without the claim of descending different adult behavior. Just keep living the lie Christians, for now it is what it is. Be mindful of the renewed mercies of God.

My military service and participation in the 1991 Desert Storm Gulf War is without a doubt or reservation the cause for my physical and mental afflictions. The military pushes and pushes to get you in the mode that best suits them. From running in combat boots for long distances on a consistent basis to lying on the ground in freezing snow and ice and being subjected to chemical agents, it's designed to push and punish the mind and body demanding a committal of the soul.

They hide that tidbit of information behind the heroism of protecting freedom and democracy. I would do it all again, but without the drumming and drilling that has caused my ailments and afflictions. I really pray and empathize for those that have to travel the route that I have to arrive at being a χριστιανός. To serve and be patriotic is honorable, but to what end does your service and patriotism gets syphoned? Ten years I served in the military and there was only one positive constant, my mother telling me often and with regularity to **"keep God first in my life."**

The instability caused by being ordered to serve at several different duty stations wreaked havoc on my desire to commit to anything other than shooting accurately and being physically and mentally prepared. With that said, I'm telling you to be a soldier for God, before soldiering for man or democracy. Foundationally speaking, you'll be better off in the long run. I always went the extra mile for the military and my career, but I neglected my relationship with the Holy Spirit.

The Holy Spirit is the green light and red light in this life of fast paced going nowhere. I'm sure it's the answer the question in life if you remember the focus of the first chapter. The evil one fired his arrows by the men that served with me. I can only remember three or four soldiers in the thousands that I worked with that proclaimed the goodness of God. That is the war that I wished I had won. If I had taken the mantle that I had been taught to love and honor and witnessed with it, big things could have been achieved for the Lord.

Gulf War issues and symptoms began to show up shortly after my return from Iraq and Desert Storm (1991). Mood swings, distant behavior, over working and chronic pain were just a taste of what was to become real and invasive. When despair replaces hope, vulgar thoughts, careless actions, timeless consideration, and inattentive living makes up our daily being. Denial of such is the standard by which the affected party lives on. That denial keeps him or her assured of functionality, when its really disaster manifested over years of chameleon rhetoric and behavior.

Hiding these feelings and ailments, became common place. It's a daily routine that builds up to an event of tragic proportions and overwhelming, mountainous issues. How long does it take? Parallel are the lifetime actions, circumstances and impending responses of a 34-year-old Christian, loose cannon with a great deal of the unknowing in my wake. Reflection of some sort would be paramount at this time. When we reflect back to a given point and time, we can see where we went wrong and by the love and grace of God, we can begin to formulate a plan for the annihilation of repetitive, denigrating behavior.

You're still looking for the dotted I's and crossed T's. Finding the incorrect punctuation is blocking the intent of the grammar. See and discover the multiple narratives of prayer, commitment, disregard, and sex in their entirety. You're just waiting for me to quote thousands of scriptures and passages from the bible, but I'm not rewriting the bible. I'm begging and trying to persuade you to learn from the path of mistakes, impulsive decisions and infidelities in life. Not just mistakes and infidelities with woman or indulgences, but the infidelities against God's word and purpose.

We accept and give special attention to the laws and rules of humankind, for example; criminal laws, social laws, football, basketball, baseball, soccer, hockey, ping pong and cliff diving rules. When it comes to laws, rules and commandments of God, we're dismissive, questioning, doubtful, denying and hateful. Recently folks have grasped a hold on the phrase "it's a hoax or misconception." We're ready to follow humankind wherever they lead without the thought of outcomes.

If not for God, anything concerning humankind wouldn't exist. The establishment of actions appropriate for social acceptance is often more important than _agape or charity._ A flaw exists in the performances and actions of humankind as it pertains to the Kingdom establishment. The Holy Trinity maybe authentically difficult to obey or be a part of, but _why would you be so against and hateful toward a concept or design of grace, love and mercy for all, to all, and of all?_ Answer that question or supposition immediately!!!

During my travels around the world I have met, greeted, hugged, kissed, had sexual intercourse and shaken hands with thousands of people from every walk of life, so many in fact, that I can't remember the vast majority of them. I've witnessed murder suicide, spousal abuse, death, all matter of crimes, injustices, drug and alcohol abuse and defective human decisions. Tragic accidents like two tour buses crashing into each other in Germany killing more than a handful of people. Military plane crashes, vehicle accidents, explosions, shooting incidents and friendly fire accidents.

Winters and summers that were so extreme everyone and everything had to remain inside and nothing was capable of movement. Car crashes that left nothing involved in the incident recognizable. I've experienced earthquakes that made beds jump up and down, and tall skyscraper buildings sway back and forth, concrete streets and sidewalks ripple like water, and also tornadoes and hurricanes. Decapitated heads dismember bodies, burned and decaying bodies, body parts just scattered around and people who found pleasure in that.

I've worked with, greeted, shaken hands, served and had conversations with men and women that committed mass murder and were labeled as serial killers, young teenagers that murdered families and other teenagers, adults that molested and killed children and I refused to consult God all in just over 30 years of living and my life was void of guidance and choice. This is why I'm writing to you now. Now is the time to reveal the **CHRISTIAN LIVING LIE**.

There are people that exist that are Satan ordained pure, instruments of evil. I had the duty to serve and cater to a couple of men that I want to introduce you to. The first being a man named Gary Ridgeway. You might know him as The Green River Killer. I shook hands with Mr. Ridgeway and provided his razor when he needed. I also served him breakfast and lunch. The evil spirit could be felt in his hand shake and in his eyes. My vain existence didn't compare to the power that Satan fueled that instrument of death with.

He murdered over fifty women in the Seattle area over a twenty-year time frame. He received a deal from the prosecutor to avoid the death penalty. Every day they would come to the jail and put a bullet proof vest with a baseball cap on him and he would lead them to different locations where he had dumped bodies. He also found pleasure in sexual acts with bodies that had been dead for days. Evil can't escape our visceral capabilities, but we fall when we deny or shun what it's indicating.

I remember this man only as Santa Claus. He portrayed Santa Claus for decades. Children even visited him at his residence so they could receive treats and attention from him. One day Santa Claus was arrested and bought up to the floor that I was working the graveyard shift on. I didn't shake Santa Claus' hand, but I looked into his eyes and had a brief conversation with him. He was a polite and respectable person. We, society, have given Santa Claus god status and we still don't understand that God wouldn't molest our children.

He molested countless number of children for decades. He molested children at his residence and at the places that he wore his Santa suit. According to the law, he was a pedophile. People unknowingly provided him their children to be molested. As children sat on his lap directly in front of parents, he molested, fingered, and groped children. Jail and prison are the most dangerous place in the world for pedophiles. Pedophiles dishonor the criminal code and they are subject to a jail and prison inmate punishment that involves several beatings, sodomizing, and ultimately death. In this case, Santa elected not to suffer such a faith. He hung himself after I did my first security check. I saw and felt the evil in his spirit and eyes. He took the Judas Iscariot way out.

Matthew 27:3-6

³ Then Judas, which had betrayed him, when he saw that he was condemned, repented himself, and brought again the thirty pieces of silver to the chief priests and elders, ⁴ Saying, I have sinned in that I have betrayed the innocent blood. And they said, What is that to us? see thou to that. ⁵ And he cast down the pieces of silver in the temple, and departed, and went and hanged himself. ⁶ And the chief priests took the silver pieces, and said, It is not lawful for to put them into the treasury, because it is the price of blood.

Both of those men added to my visceral experience. For decades, I have had to decipher what is being said to discover what isn't being said and most of all what is being said to say something else. This is vital in assisting χριστιανός, because far too many times when we have spiritual or carnal issues, we choose to hide our discomfort and we desire to maintain our preference to remain anonymous. Who wants to let the world know that they murdered multiple women and did grotesque things with their dead corpses? Who wants to admit to touching and violating little children? To gain exposure to these types of people heightens the need and presence of prayer.

When χριστιανός choose to go back to their spiritual roots the acts and experiences follow them. The stigmatism and labeling from those around them and from the victimized are usually a mountain too high to climb. The Christian's life has been filled with a diverse abundance of worldly actions that ethical dilemmas and decisions now are being made on a shaky foundation and a spirit of uncertainty. The Christian wants to accept guidance and choice, but it's difficult when the trees can't be seen for the forest, well you know what I mean. At this point with my faith stabilized, I'll deal with my afflictions and spiritual ailments while ushering in change and development. It's a process.

Hebrews 11:24-27

24 By faith Moses, when he was come to years, refused to be called the son of Pharaoh's daughter; 25 Choosing rather to suffer affliction with the people of God, than to enjoy the pleasures of sin for a season; 26 Esteeming the reproach of Christ greater riches than the treasures in Egypt: for he had respect unto the recompence of the

reward. ²⁷ By faith he forsook Egypt, not fearing the wrath of the king: for he endured, as seeing him who is invisible.

Chapter 15: A Father with Hope

I'm sitting at work in King County Jail in Seattle Washington on the graveyard shift and somewhere around 12:30am ish, a thought and spirit of spending time with Marvin Jr. came to me. A moment in time as a father that was at the peak of my hope, so I called the Captain, and requested to be relieved because I didn't feel well. After being relieved at 1:15am ish, I went to Baby Mama's apartment and I let myself in. The hallway light was on and suddenly Baby Mama ran from her room and met me in the hallway completely naked.

She acted awkwardly and as if she didn't want me to go past that point. The shower was on and it suddenly stopped. Her ex-husband appears in a towel and I said cool, I'm just going to take Marvin Jr. and spend some time with him. I will return him day after tomorrow. She disagreed, but I grabbed him and the baby bag anyway. As I was walking toward the door, her ex-husband grabbed my arm trying to stop me from leaving with Marvin Jr. That was the same arm that I had my hand on my gun with! I threatened to harm him if he didn't release my arm.

I was extremely serious about spending time with Marvin Jr. and her ex-husband was only a moment from being shot. My hope as a father seemed to be tarnished due largely in part because of the foundation of which it existed. When I got Marvin Jr. situated in the car, I sat in the driver's seat and Baby Mama jumped in the car completely naked. I asked her to exit the car and she wouldn't, so I drove off with her in the passenger seat. When we arrived where I was living, I removed Marvin Jr. from the car and I asked one of the people that I was living with to take Marvin Jr. in the house.

That started a wrestling match between myself and Baby Mama. Yes, at 2:30am, I was wrestling with the naked mother of my oldest son in the front yard of a home in Seattle Washington at which I resided. I separated her away from me enough to get to the door of the house and I entered the house and left her outside. She knocked and requested me to return Marvin Jr. to her but I didn't respond. I didn't know then and I still don't know as of this moment how she made it home to her apartment.

At 6:00am that same morning, I received a phone call from my attorney. She said the Judge wanted me and Marvin Jr. in the courtroom at

9:00am that day, and if I didn't show up that he was going to put a warrant out for my arrest. The Judge asked me what was I thinking and said that I was bordering the boundaries of a kidnapper and that if I tried that again that he would lock me up! This may seem to be such an awful time, but in essence it portrayed me as a father who had great intentions for raising and caring for his son. My hope as a father was under attack, but it felt great because I did the right thing showing her how much I loved our son and possessing the passion to be a father to him!!!

GOD KNOWS YOUR NAME!

So much has transpired and so much philandering, transgression, indulgence, iniquity and abandonment have occurred, that a people, imposed moniker is our ultimate accusation. Where can we go from here? The trials are not any easier and the battle is waged from multiple avenues. The approaches from Lucifer himself haven't yet come to fruition. Watch what happens from this vantage point.

After my second divorce, I became a father to my two sons, Marvin Jr. and Trenton. I spent time with them, cooked, cleaned and adventured while showing them that I loved them and how much God loved them as well. The church was on my mind, but I still rejected the notion of returning even thou darkness and pain blocked my way. I began to teach my children about God and how to be men. If the weekends that I had my sons would've never expired, then I guess I would also live what I was teaching. Since that wasn't the case, let me continue on with this common or pragmatic view of this **CHRISTIAN LIVING** *the* **CHRISTIAN LIVING LIE**.

GOD KNOWS YOUR NAME!

I had stopped stealing, gambling, doing dope, drinking and lying to an extent. I possessed this false since of nobility. A partial pat on the back is what it was. Spending time loving and teaching my children gave me a since of purpose, but the truth of what I truly was would remain a **CHRISTIAN LIVING LIE**. I would still make the annual visit to my father's grave in Opelousas, and have these meritless conversations with nothing there.

Anger would manifest within me in these conversations, because I convinced myself that life as I knew it was somehow his fault. Christian upbringing was clearly out the window at this point. How could I be 35 years old and be so misguided? *Ain't that what Christians do?* We live lies, create a spiritual picture for others to see, and stand by our conviction to be a dead fool. I recall giving some folks that I associated with the opportunity to be a mainstay in my life, but they all turned out to be partially what it took to ride this path with me. Whether it was a friend that promised to help me get established in a new city or women that said they wanted to love and take care of me and my children, they didn't know what all that entailed.

Not only did I have Christian standards with my requirements on the subject, I still lied and thirst for the pleasure of several women for which I had to lie to someone else in order to be with them. Men with these issues aren't necessarily sexual deviants. For me, it was the euphoria, power, and conquering associated with the act. I didn't make a conscience decision to live this way, and I also didn't take into account the lives that I would disrupt and damage. I never approached or harmed a child. *So please picture complicit adults in our actions.* That's right Christians; we need to think twice and critically about where we're going and how we're getting there. Some call it counting the costs and others may say try it by or in the fire.

From my living, I witnessed the actions and life experiences of several hundreds of other men, women, children and families. With the knowledge of all these different scenarios, I could easily create a soap opera of epic proportion, but I chose to write this book. Maybe you have life experiences or have seen and have done some things, but not on the scale of time, atmosphere and real estate that I'm referencing. The folks I've worked and lived with led common lives with a hint of drama, and maybe some infidelity coupled with damaging habits.

I just had to exceed those standards and go for the traumatic drama. I've chosen to make a guide and helpful tool for those of us that will travel the same path or for those that want to avoid this path. That's why I've included the words; effervescent, propensity, patience, persistence, time, nothing to lose, pragmatic, indulgence, adolescence, atrocity, debauchery and despair. These words and accusations are the blueprint for Satan's lethal assailants. Ask yourselves, do you know him or her?

Falling for me was never ending. I tried so candidly to engulf myself and time in work, reflection, and hobbies. The more we try as Christians to live right is the more we, as the Apostle Paul put it, flop. A single man with a beautiful 3 bedrooms, 3 car garage, large living area home with a breath-taking view of Mount Rainier, and a well-paying job, otherwise; known as Satan's lethal assailant was the it factors. 399 26th Avenue Milton, Washington became much more of a palace of whoremongering than 113 C. Alley in Opelousas, Louisiana ever was. I was clearly beyond promiscuous and now I'm armed and seasoned.

Without the consideration of where any of my actions may lead, I proceeded to add to my recourse and rhetoric. The recourse was to go back to those actions with those that I had put in the past. You see some folks still held on to the hope of pleasing and keeping me. The rhetoric was amped up because my status and stature had changed. Remember, this is the nineties when a man with a job and benefits was still a subject worth pursuing even by the most successful women of the world!

As I think about recourse and rhetoric, my closest brother comes to my mind, because he did the same thing. These are the brothers from which I had to learn how to be a man and who taught them how to be men, because daddy was dead in the grave, unknown, or just absentee. This is what I failed to realize. Humankind always seeks and reverts back to what felt or feels good.

GOD KNOWS YOUR NAME!

When Christians as χριστιανόςs, apply this notion or concept to their lives, they seek the guidance and choice of the Holy Spirit. Others of us wallow in sin and the flesh feeding tendencies. Fight and stay in the race with Olympic prowess by seeking the guidance of the Holy Spirit. Be a χριστιανός that chooses good rather than evil. Don't try to make it appear, seem or sound like I'm professing or preaching perfection, I'm talking about a course of action that secures a certain type of reward in an eternal state. Perfection isn't ours to award.

Prior to my second marriage which began with *Henry (Hank) Cannon* telling me to let the gurl out the closet, I always helped my family and relatives financially when I was able to, but over the course of the years that charity and love began to be shunned upon, scrutinized, and discouraged. My relationship with my first son faltered and my attempts to get back into the church seemed pointless.   What was preventing me from excelling or ascending to the next level or as Richard Rohr put it "the second half of life?"

Marriage shouldn't be a step back or a hindrance. PLEASE DON'T MARRY THE GURL TO LET HER OUT OF THE CLOSET!!! Pillow talk can be a powerful persuader if used with the proper precision, especially in the absence of guidance and choice. The lesson here is for men to be men that guide and love their families according to the Word of God. A family absent of charity is a family absent of the charity of God.

Can you see what's preventing the spiritual chips from falling? A poison had been administered and the anti-venom was hidden in plain sight. The Word of God tells us to cut off the opposite body part which offends or disobeys His truth. We as χριστιανός are to see and apply that to our daily lives with practicality and seek to keep our families on a common goal of charity, which means LOVE, for all.

I can't begin to tell all as the beginning of the book seemed it would do, because we don't forgive as God forgives. On a separate note, I have a rhetorical question. If God forgives and forgets as some of us believe, why are we judged at a later time for what He has forgiven and forgotten? I reached back in time, and sought another chance with love in Sparkle.

Do you remember Sparkle, my first true, heart, given love from 1987 before I left Ft. Lewis, Washington to go to Germany? The problem was that now I unknowingly and sub-consciously loved another woman at this point almost fourteen years later. Sparkle and I seemed to be in tuned with one another and the circumstances for both of our lives were such that the availability couldn't have been scripted any better.

I divorced, and her freshly broken up with a boyfriend, could you ask for better timing? At this point, I was a bit timid about love and relationships, because my indulgences and cold demeanor may have caused someone to try to commit suicide. Four bottles of pills had been ingested by the time I noticed the change in behavior. That attempt had me walking on egg shells for a minute, because my older brother's successful suicide was still on my heart.

At the same time, I also encountered a fatal attraction due to my indulgences. The situation was so heightened that I had to go to my supervisor and indicate that I might have to kill this individual.

Strange occurrences began to take place in my life and the life of my girlfriend at the time. I think every sexual predator should have at least one fatal attraction. Back to Sparkle and my love for someone else.

I wanted to pick up right where Sparkle and I had left off. That was a problem for Sparkle because she really took her recent break up very hard. Listen up, the focused and insensitive type, if love isn't reciprocated, then it probably isn't love that two people have for each other. That conversation and the following sex that Sparkle and I had exposed my love for someone else. I would never ever be able to show that person how much I truly loved and cared for her, because someone was already doing that. I wanted him to die, disappear or just mess it up bad, or make an unforgiveable mistake.

Because of this love, I couldn't understand Sparkles issues or circumstances, so I avoided and ignored her. I felt betrayed by her, and so it is, our time and window had passed. Now I needed to ask myself, how did you get to a point where you want some one's husband to die, me with my propensity, patience, persistence, time and nothing to lose. The Devil just loved the hell out of me at this point, and there is no need to wonder who was the love that I could never have she is the same love that you could never have.

I pursued that man's wife. We even committed adultery. She tasted so sweet to me that I wanted to kidnap her and take her far away from anyone and anything. I confused her with glorious rhetoric and future tenses on all levels of satisfaction and happiness. The tarnished is always seeking to tarnish someone else. She began to question her life and love putting her children's future and upbringing in jeopardy and the scrutiny from family and friends would've been catastrophic. She would've had to live with a burning question, will God ever forgive me?

Although I truly loved her, this was wrong, sinful and against all that she had prayed for. The more she prayed for forgiveness was the more I confused her. There's something about redemptive power. My relentless pursuit began to let up and I backed off, but kept in touch. Maybe there's hope for me yet I thought. I really believe that in life it's possible to love more than once. We choose to love others that may not reciprocate that love or have to grow into loving us in return, but it's all good if it's in God's Will.

I should've hired someone to do damage control in the life that I was living and the trail of detrimental issues that I deposited into women's lives. My vain actions and meritless behavior were without rhyme or reason. It seems that no matter how I try to explain it, it's beyond comprehension. We can't really begin to grasp how much we've scarred or hurt people until we peer at life through spiritual eyes.

I'm talking about the scars that cause love, trust, abandonment, separation and sexual issues. That stuff that eats away at our spiritual fiber to the core. We, χριστιανόςs, have to change the moniker and the narrative while focusing on the heart and soul. You'll hear more about this particular topic a little later on as this unfolds. Thru it all, my hope as a father was getting stronger and more convicted by the Word of GOD!!! The entire process was leading me into understanding and knowing that my hope as a man and a father should be in the resurrection of our Lord and Savior, Jesus Christ!!!

Chapter 16: A Battle of The Causes

At this point, I have truly given my heart and love to two women and it hasn't worked out for me and love. For some reason, I decided to take a glance back at some of my indulgences. I tried to have more sex than Wilt Chamberlain claimed to have had with more nationalities of women than he had claimed to have had. I fornicated and committed adultery and swam in it. I cheated, stole, lied, gambled divorced twice, drank, did drugs, scarred women, and hurt families, the nice dog, the rhetoric chameleon and the list probably shouldn't stop there. What was the reason for this look back or overview if I may call it that? That really needed to be answered, but I ignored it. Thank God for His new mercies. **You're witnessing the beginning of spirit versus flesh.**

Galatians 5:15-17 (NIV)

15 If you bite and devour each other, watch out or you will be destroyed by each other. **16** So I say, walk by the Spirit, and you will not gratify the desires of the flesh. **17** For the flesh desires what is contrary to the Spirit, and the Spirit what is contrary to the flesh. They are in conflict with each other, so that you are not to do whatever you want.

I've seen and witnessed all manner of things in my living and the living of others. Folks have been convicted in the court of law for crimes from bestiality to murder. The depravity of humankind has shown its ugly outcome. Humankind as a whole has become insensitive, in-compassionate, irresponsible, intolerant, and incapable. It's bordering a Sodom and Gomorrah situation that all of us need to pay close attention to avoid the wrath for such principles and behaviors. Read Chapter 19 in the book of Genesis to gain the knowledge contained in the instructions and outcomes. At this point, I want to just remind all of us about the commandment of God contained in Chapter 18 of Leviticus. Reading these two chapters and understanding the depravity of humankind is vital to our efforts and prayers for forgiveness and our dedication to repent. No words exist more powerful than I am The LORD Thy GOD!!

When we have created issues and trouble for ourselves and other people have been victimized by our actions, we cause them to formulate a defense against us and those that appear to be like us or even those that may not look like or be like us at all. This defense is at a deeply rooted personal level and is unrivaled by any other emotional reaction or guarded feeling. So, what can we expect now from this position that we have caused and created, when we want to right the ship, so to speak, or pursue a new path?

This is the point in life where I, me personally, had to start screaming God, Jesus and the Holy Spirit inwardly and outwardly. Who would begin to believe that I was a χριστιανός? Isn't that what other Christians do, doubt other Christians? At this moment, I found joy in being a good father to my children and shielding them away from my iniquities and transgressions.

Do you remember that I'm a 1991 Gulf War Veteran? I almost forgot until depression found its mark and another veteran that worked with me noticed how much overtime I worked. 15 years later enter stage left, PTSD. Post-Traumatic Stress Disorder not as bad as it sounds, and is quite common, but quietly dealt with amongst the medical and psychological professions. Again, I am the scapegoat putting me out there, so others can be liberated, freed, empowered, inspired and informed.

GOD KNOWS YOUR NAME!

Car accidents, rape victims, suicide witnesses, murder witnesses, combat soldiers and many more are examples of people who live with PTSD. The forces of life and evil become more than we can bear. We're shamed and embarrassed by this position in life, so we drown as we push away from the docks and shores of truth. Denial hurts a great number of people. Denying our Lord and Savior, Jesus the Christ adds to the tumultuous times that we all must exist in and live through.

I had to learn what this thing, PTSD, was and how it functions. It's common and more of us are affected by it than we care to admit. At first, denial of the fact caused me more detriment, than the issue itself. The end result wasn't very clear or conclusive. The struggle to understand the problem and where it was about to take me was the most difficult time for me. At this point, I arrogantly acted as if I had things figured out.

I focused on getting ahead in life, and worked on becoming financially free. After 18 months of 2-3 times a week of conversation and probing, the answer to helping the situation, but not rid me of the issue, was to STOP. Stop caring, working, thinking, talking, stressing, hearing, seeing, listening and get someone to pay the bills and manage your finances if possible and you can continue to be a father up to a certain extent. STOP.

What does a χριστιανός do when presented with such circumstances? I'm not asking you. I presented this question to myself. I worked more overtime at the jail than regular hours for years. How was I going to fill that hole and void in my life, when the instructions were not to fill it or even think about it? The help is in the hole and you should dive head first and submerge yourself as deep as possible. Broken, wounded, sad, stripped and confused, I asked the Lord a question. Where to from here? That question resembles prayer to me y'all.

Sure, you want me to give you the answer and hear about the miraculous change and make over, but don't be so naïve. That's not how it works, especially if you want it when you want it. My cousin, the late Clarence Dunbar Sr., believed we'll all get the answers to our cares, concerns and dilemmas when time is complete and I agree.

GOD KNOWS YOUR NAME!

Stop, Dwight's order, presented me with some difficult challenges, but I followed the instructions from my therapist and doctors to the letter. I found my prayer life in the process. Still armed with propensity, patience, more time, persistence and nothing to lose, I lived carefree and treated others without a thought of their destination or how I affected that direction.

<u>The 16th President of the United States of America, Abraham Lincoln said this:</u>

"With malice toward none, with charity for all, with firmness in the right as God gives us to see the right, let us strive on to finish the work we are in, to bind up the nation's wounds, to care for him who shall have borne the battle and for his widow, and his orphan, to do all which may achieve and cherish a just and lasting peace among ourselves and with all nations."

It's distinctively clear to me now why he believed that the above statement should be carried out to the fullest and passionate capabilities of America. He also recognized as I do that <u>*nobody wins in a war and war changes a man.*</u> Approximately 22 veterans commit suicide daily if my information is correct. The issue is real and present. If we have offered our service to our country for the preservation of freedom and democracy, then what should our service to God entail?

When I connect my spirit to the Word of God and the challenges and adversities that are put before me, I am sort of prepared from Abraham Lincoln's quote. We have to deal with challenges and adversities in two manners. Spiritually and carnally, we must navigate through the evil and maintain our positive ascension and pray against our negative descension.

God knows that this is a virtual impossibility, so He offers us the blood and path of Jesus Christ. God's plan gave the vision and spirit to Abraham Lincoln, because God cares for us whom he is well pleased with. With knowing that God cares and loves us in this manner, we should live the entirety of our days in humble submission and servitude. From this point, I had to proceed with my instruction to put life and responsibility on temporary hold for now.

1 Peter 1:1-5

Peter, an apostle of Jesus Christ, to the strangers scattered throughout Pontus, Galatia, Cappadocia, Asia, and Bithynia, ² Elect according to the foreknowledge of

God the Father, through sanctification of the Spirit, unto obedience and sprinkling of the blood of Jesus Christ: Grace unto you, and peace, be multiplied. ³ Blessed be the God and Father of our Lord Jesus Christ, which according to his abundant mercy hath begotten us again unto a lively hope by the resurrection of Jesus Christ from the dead, ⁴ To an inheritance incorruptible, and undefiled, and that fadeth not away, reserved in heaven for you, ⁵ Who are kept by the power of God through faith unto salvation ready to be revealed in the last time.

I played video games, golf, chess, shopped, watched movies, built a shed, exercised a little, fornicated a lot, and then I was told that that may very well be my life for the rest of my life. For seventeen years and through the adolescent ages, the personal teaching and encouragement from Evelyn Andrus was to work hard and be responsible. How was I supposed to chisel through that? The answer came from her.

When I explained the situation and illness to her, she said, "Just pray and take care of yourself baby." "Do whatever it is that they tell you to do, because I'm sure they know better." She gave me credit for the years and work that I had already put in and said that I had done my best to be a productive member of society, and a Christian. No guilt can be placed on you. She also raised us in the ways of the Lord. Just what I needed when I needed it, you rock Mama.

In 2003, I attended my 20th year High School Class Reunion after missing the 10 year reunion. It was great to see how all of us had become adults, and was living to become who God intended us to become in theory. There were more than a handful of us that had passed away. If you're still living in the here and now, then God is still molding and making. During that weekend, I visited my father's grave again with disdain and questions to which I may never know the answer.

I paid particular attention to two women, in my 1983 classmates, for the weekend in Opelousas. I returned to Seattle with their phone numbers and I communicated with them on a regular basis. Not thinking of anything permanent or committed, I enjoyed the conversations and sharing with both of them. I sent flowers and well wishes and showered them with compliments and the sly smile of course. Since they already knew my family and upbringing, my position in the hopeful candidate area was elevated, but that hadn't struck me yet.

A Christian in limbo is a Christian with propensity, patience, time, persistence, effervescence and nothing to lose. These ladies should have been privy to that information as we all should and we need to stop letting personalities disrupt and derail our life's focus and assignment. Since we don't understand that authentic love is never-ending, relationships continue to go on lacking in trust and commitment. Marriage is vital for the institution of God's family. Marriage is not a frivolous undertaking that you mention in a punch line. I failed on all levels of flesh, spirit, and word to understand and honor that fact. Time after time, I walked away from wives or provided no emotional content for them to access or confront. That carnage of time in my life reciprocated and fueled itself, a self-sustaining carnage that I arrogantly and ignorantly embraced.

GOD KNOWS YOUR NAME!

I made a concerted effort to pray for deliverance from that plague, but prayer must be done in spirit and in truth. I've got a long way to go. We all could accurately begin the institution of marriage by consulting the Holy Spirit and having the love for your wife that leads to the devotion to die for her. Men you only need her respect, so earn it. God knows the intention and truth of our hearts and desires. It's imperative that we honor and respect that as it concerns our relationships in marriage. For all of our mischief and oddities, we only get ignored.

Ephesians 5:32-33 (NIV)

[32] This is a profound mystery—but I am talking about Christ and the church. [33] However, each one of you also must love his wife as he loves himself, and the wife must respect her husband.

Chapter 17: Aimlessly Fueling the Flames

Now back in Milton, Washington, I had returned from my visit home and my father's grave. It was time to redeem the lost time with a few of the ladies on standby. My children had to get some times as well. Notice the order that I put the two in. Some folks would like you to believe that a zebra can't change its strips, but they want you to change yours when it benefits them. If you're dazzled by such lame babbling, then such is the path that you're choosing to go down. For it is that lame babble, such as this, that Christians like myself that were very well versed and knowledgeable.

Everything about me showed these characteristics: complimentary, polite, giving, caring, humble, strong, delicate, patient, compassionate, dependable and serious. Who doesn't notice those, and who turns a blind eye to those, and who walks away from those surface level characteristics? All of those characteristics are where the predator in us as human beings' dwell and rest. I say today that we should be on the lookout for the heart, spirit, and motive in people. God's presence and promise!!!

Matthew 7:14-16

¹⁴ Because strait is the gate, and narrow is the way, which leadeth unto life, and few there be that find it. ¹⁵ Beware of false prophets, which come to you in sheep's clothing, but inwardly they are ravening wolves. ¹⁶ Ye shall know them by their fruits. Do men gather grapes of thorns, or figs of thistles?

GOD KNOWS YOUR NAME!

We're not monsters because of this behavior. We're just absent of a positive thought process. The vain existence has no goals or motives, so where do we direct our opinions and objections? The answer is in placing our faith and trust where it deserves such distinction. Try it in and by the fire.

1 Peter 1:6-8

⁶ Wherein ye greatly rejoice, though now for a season, if need be, ye are in heaviness through manifold temptations: ⁷ That the trial of your faith, being much more precious than of gold that perisheth, though it be

tried with fire, might be found unto praise and honour and glory at the appearing of Jesus Christ: **8** Whom having not seen, ye love; in whom, though now ye see him not, yet believing, ye rejoice with joy unspeakable and full of glory:

This is the common and pragmatic view. This doesn't come from a Harvard or Stanford education. In fact, it comes from a 12th grade and street education. You won't find more than a handful of quotes from the great authors in this autobiography, slash tell all, slash teach all shocker. I have to give this to you in spirit and in truth, otherwise; what's the point. It has to be worth more than the paper it's written on and has to come from a χριστιανός.

I want you to see that it's just a common man, a simple man, that has infiltrated the hearts and emotions of several hundreds if not thousands of people and created havoc, instability, disdain, confusion and debauchery. It only takes the assault on a few to reach the feelings and emotions of many! My vain existence and **CHRISTIAN LIVING LIE** won't make World News, Good Morning America, 20/20, 48 Hours, CNN's Situation Room, nor Oprah's Super Soul Sunday, but it had the impact of any story of hurt or betrayal that you'll ever see on those programs. What has your **CHRISTIAN LIVING LIE** accomplished? Please, answer that question with regularity sooner rather than later.

Personally, and publicly, I have apologized and asked for forgiveness from those that I have affected directly and indirectly. The negative impact previously listed is ongoing, even thou, the culprit is decades removed and forgiven by the only forgiveness that he is garnered by his propensity and commitment to worship God in spirit and in truth as a χριστιανός. To my GOD, I have begged, cried, and pledged to continue on this path of healing and reconciliation. I bear strong and visible witness to the palm retentive attention and affection of my God.

GOD KNOWS YOUR NAME!

The real or true χριστιανός sustains sympathy, compassion, empathy, and compathy. These characteristics don't invade or confuse the spirit of a χριστιανός. When confronted with this situation, it's best to error on the side of protecting our virtues. Without a doubt, I know that my worth and value is in the eyes, hands, grace, and love of the BEHOLDER / JEHOVAH.

While some thought for my well-being that I should stop, and put life on hold, the drama over child visitation and baby mama drama said I don't think so. Court appearances and the constant barrage of motions and accusations were never ending and financially burdensome. My, "I can just walk away," attitude and belief ushered in a separation from my second wife which made her bitter and angry at me.

In the shadow of this situation, I felt free to indirectly mislead an unwilling target. I floated around and laid my head here and there. I even slept in my truck and the locker room at work on a few occasions. That behavior went on for months and when the unwilling target realized that I was in that predicament she opened her door to me. Sleeping on the coach allowing her children to become emotionally and spiritually attached to me while on occasion helping them deal with their dying husband and father in the bedroom not far away, wasn't good enough for me. Can you see or realize that nothing or no one was off limits to me. Before he died and while he was lying on a bed in the house, I had sex with her in the next room and hot tub sex every other night and she treated me and cared for me like I was her husband. We, her and her children functioned like a family, but that wasn't a long-term consideration, focus, feeling, or thought for me.

Nothing was a long-term consideration for me, and I was a Bastard for hurting them the way that I did. One of her children apparently saw what they couldn't or wasn't willing to see. From the moment I arrived, she profanely rejected my presence and condemned her mother for inviting me in the house. How could you, I remember her saying. Are you some kind of desperate whore she screamed in agony? Daynay was the older woman and she wasn't desperate. She tried to change the narrative in my life with the hope that I could find refuge, togetherness, and peace in a relationship with her. We were not on the same page or sheet of music!

God help me, I should have departed from their presence and sought other means of shelter. How long does it take? On occasions, adults' consent to situations and issues for their own satisfaction or gain. Complicit is the word we're looking for. I'm not using complicity as a pardon for my promiscuity or infidelity and more importantly, I take ownership of my behavior. Watch what else I had to own.

In the jail, I conducted a security check on the mental, medical unit. I observed an inmate lying in the middle of his cell on the floor. His skin complexion was blue, so I knew that he was unconscious and not breathing. The code and emergency calls were made and the medical staff began their efforts to resuscitate him. They discovered something blocking his airway. He had managed to tear his mattress open and had eaten the stuffing from the mattress. He was revived and stood trial for the killing of his father, mother, girlfriend, and two Canadian Police Officers. They found him guilty and sentenced him to death.

One morning during breakfast at 6:45am on the 10th Floor of the jail an inmate came out of his cell on the upper level. He climbed on top of the railing and said, "goodnight boys." He did a head first swan dive breaking his neck and killing himself on contact. How long does it take may have been plaquing his spirit and life as well.

During the graveyard shift at King County Corrections Facility, an "officer needs help" call rang throughout the building. When we arrived at the location that the officer called for help from, I observed a man acting erratic and confused. In one leap from a standing position, he jumped approximately 8 - 10 feet over 2 beds that were side by side. The gentleman wasn't responding to any of the commands that were being given by the sergeant and we had to act swiftly to prevent him from hurting himself or others.

The sergeant ordered the door to be opened so we could go in the dorm and secure the gentleman. When the door opened, he charged toward us which ultimately led to us struggling with the gentleman just outside of the door. The struggle went to the ground and at this point approximately 8 officers were in an extremely violent situation and weren't having any success at restraining the inmate. The sergeant used pepper spray and it had no effect on the inmate. Suddenly after a feverish physical struggle with several different restraint techniques and basic securing positions the inmate's body went limp as if he wasn't even there. The situation quickly went from officer needs help to inmate needs medical staff.

We stood and watched in disbelief as the medical staff examined and started life restoring CPR while other staff called for EMS and the ambulance. Upon arrival at the hospital, they pronounced the inmate dead and that started the ball rolling for the tensest year of my life. Not only did the inmate's family threaten to retaliate against every officer involved, the jail and state started an inquest into the death of the inmate which could mean prison time for officers if negligent or criminal behavior is proven.

After holding our breath for 18 months, the coroner/medical examiner reported that the inmate's heart had exploded in his chest cavity due to the ingestion of a massive amount of heroin and crack cocaine. The gentleman had been arrested a day earlier for drug distribution and had swallowed several little balloon packages of the drugs to avoid arrest. The balloons ruptured that evening causing the whole episode and the explosion of his heart. We were cleared of any wrong doing and responsibility for his death. My spirit couldn't help but to feel that I had killed that man. We were exonerated by man, but God was the exonerator that we needed.

In my **CHRISTIAN LIVING LIE**, I was just as troubled and dead as those examples that I just shared with you!!! **HELLO** The toughest times that we go through in life is when we transcend from not caring to caring. My vain existence had its moments of defeat, granger and mystery. The majority of our choices lead to disaster if we choose the way we feel or see that life ought to be.

I'm still a father to two sons at this point. My sons have a father that they truly didn't know. I had considered them in my actions, so they haven't witnessed my heart and spirit torturing of people up to this point. Through it all, I continued to spend time with them, but not on a meaningful scale. The distance between where each of them lived was about a one-hour drive with minimal traffic.

The driving time from my location to either of them was a little more than an hour, so do the math and the geography and you'll see that the majority of my weekend visits with them was driving on the freeway picking them up and bringing them back home. I was tired and overwhelmed and they didn't deserve a father that bought them into this mess. I was tired and overwhelmed, because I started kicking myself for being a father from irresponsible actions.

Despair, depression and a desire to end my life was the result. The cell phone rang and it was Dwight. Hello Marvin how are you doing he asked? I feel like shit Dwight. Why? I just dropped off my youngest son and he grabbed me around my neck screaming, hollering, and refusing to go to his mother. As I walked away, he was pushing, hitting and kicking trying to get out of her arms. Marvin, that's just a true dose of reality, life isn't life without it. He always said something from psych 101 that made sense to me disrupting and derailing the current thought processes.

The relationship with my children is none existent at the moment. Bitterness, anger, parenting differences and geography from my decision to relocate to Louisiana to care for my elderly disabled mother gave Satan the opportunity to divide and distort. My children know that I'm their father and if God has His way the children always come back to the father!!! I must admit that life without a relationship with my children has been bleak on occasions, but I continue to trust God and His way in this.

A couple of years into my employment at the jail, I became sexually involved with a few white female employees one of which I married, but I'm only going to discuss a certain relationship, because of the foundation that it was based on and its 14 year existence. You will know her as Daynay. I say sexually involved, but subconsciously this escapade was much more than that. She never tried to keep me from my sinful nature or the propensity as such, and she was definitely in my corner.

If I had a bad day at work, Daynay would listen and try to understand the situation. If I had an argument or disagreement with a wife or girlfriend, Daynay would show me a smile and a gentle spirit. Whenever I pounded my chest and left home disappointed with a wife, Daynay invited me in and had untamed vigorous sex and made love to me. Yes, we made love on occasions. We talked and communicated like two adults on the same path in life, but it was revealed to me that Daynay didn't know God or His deity.

For 14 years until I moved to Louisiana with no plans to return, Daynay loved fed, shared, showered, dated, consoled, celebrated, cared for and coddled me. _Please tell me that you see the calamity and toxicity in our behavior._ For 14 years, not one disagreement, argument, denial of sex, difference in opinion or mention of our wrong doing. Even after I accepted my call to the ministry of Christ, I let Satan use me in that relationship.

Even if I stayed away for months or a half of a year in fact, I could walk right in as if I never left. Daynay never had other relationships that she didn't make step aside or be removed for us to fornicate with each other and I would stay with her for days or a week on occasion. I cannot stress guidance and choice enough. I'm so joyous that the LORD didn't remove His hand from me in that span of time. Y'all, we have to count the cost plain and simple.

Romans 1:27-29

[27] And likewise also the men, leaving the natural use of the woman, burned in their lust one toward another; men with men working that which is unseemly, and receiving in themselves that recompence of their error which was meet. [28] And even as they did not like to retain God in their knowledge, God gave them over to a reprobate mind, to do those things which are not convenient; [29] Being filled with all unrighteousness, fornication, wickedness, covetousness, maliciousness; full of envy, murder, debate, deceit, malignity; whisperers,

While I was proclaiming the gospel, sleeping with Danay, crushing another woman's heart and family, Baby Mama, Malaysia, Lawsuit, and a few others that thought their mold didn't have any fractures, cracks, or leaks, I was simultaneously communicating and flattering the two women from my class reunion. The one didn't know about the other, but what jerk tells one about another? I would be that jerk and I did it on more than one occasion. The classmate that I had been friends with and grew up fairly close to would be the one to pay me a visit at my home in Milton, WA, and eventually, we would get married. At the time of her visit my mother was living me. **Houston there is a problem.**

In a conversation just a day before the visit was to happen, my mother said this, "a new broom always sweeps good." What? Needless to say, the relationship that I was about to embark on was tainted. My mother could not stand the woman and the woman ignored my mother for that week. Mama decided to leave my home in Milton and return to Louisiana. In came the new bride and the sudden need to bicker about my mother amongst other things. When our problems first started, I just tried to ignore them, but as they progressed and intensified, I would leave and slide under Daynay. If I returned and the situation remained, I went back to Daynay for a night or two. This wasn't a Denmark, or Las Vegas wedding, but I still possessed the walk away attitude.

This was my third marriage and it's about to take a drastic direction because of an impulsive decision. I started to feel as though my calling to the ministry of Christ was tainted and was a hoax as some would put it. Falling short on a daily and consistent basis consumed me and it was difficult for me to try to understand what my wife was experiencing or struggling to get past. She had several issues and desires that I couldn't line up with, so our relationship started taking Satanic blows on a seriously, destructive scale.

All of this made me feel inadequate as a man and husband, so I lashed out in retaliation letting anger and frustration determine my responses. I really couldn't imagine that I would be in the courthouse filing for another divorce, not when I consulted with God and asked Him to choose my wife for me. I say consulted because it wasn't the spiritual conversation and prayer that I should've given unto God, Jesus Christ, and The Holy Ghost. When our divorce was finalized, the court had awarded me the house and all of the items that were there before she moved to Milton from Opelousas. At that time, I asked her to leave my residence.

Prior to this point several conversations had taken place about our relationship being over and that she should be trying to find somewhere else to stay or return to Opelousas. When I asked her to leave my residence, she disagreed and that prompted me to call the police. After over an hour of back and forth, the officer told me that he couldn't make her leave, because she had established residence, meaning she had items in the home.

I told him, "Officer if you leave, I'm just going to call you back." He said "officer Andrus if I have to come back here then someone is going to jail." "I should tell you that the lady has her children in there and if she or they say that you did something I don't have to tell you what's next." At that point I told a lie and said she pushed me, causing the officer to have to arrest her. The officer pleaded with me not to do this. He suggested to me, just leave and come back after a while or use the courts to handle this. I was adamant "she pushed me." I had her arrested from a lie that I told. It didn't bother me because we talked for months two or three times a day about where we were in life and our spiritual relationship with the LORD. She spoke awesome about The Lord and the children quoted scriptures from the bible. She had a church addendum, and work ethic that manifested after she moved to Milton from Opelousas.

While she sat in jail, I removed all of her items from my residence and bought the children to school the next day and someone would pick them up from there. Not my finest hour Y'all!!! Later I submitted a letter to the District Attorney, recanting my story and acknowledged that I lied to the police for the purposes of ending the situation.   To what end would we go with our cruel treatment toward others? Neither charity nor love had any part in that relationship from the start. Foundation is all I can say. We need to know the purpose of marriage and the role it performs in God's plan. In that instance, my moral compass was on a true east, but the adversary had other plans for the person that was to be the Help Meet.

Genesis 2:18

And the Lord God said, It is not good that the man should be alone; I will make him an help meet for him.

Chapter 18: If You Desire the Truth

Sexually transmitted diseases, depression, car accidents, 3 divorces, Suicidal thoughts, military career ended, pressured abortions, adultery, Gulf War Syndrome, PTSD, lying, stealing, gambling, dope smoking, victimizing people mentally and physically, child out of wedlock, falsified character, reckless, predator, unstable, selfish, fatal attraction, brushes with death, and Satan's devil are some and certainly not a complete list of my many propensities, indulgences, and sinful behaviors.

This list began to take form when I was nine years old. I was the third son born to a married man and woman, but I would grow to live the life of a bastard in the sight of the Lord, for if we're not His children then we are bastards.

Deuteronomy 23:2-3

[2] A bastard shall not enter into the congregation of the Lord; even to his tenth generation shall he not enter into the congregation of the Lord. [3] An Ammonite or Moabite shall not enter into the congregation of the Lord; even to their tenth generation shall they not enter into the congregation of the Lord for ever:

I refused to seek, receive and understand God's chastisement for my vain actions. For a preacher, this is a great deal to overcome and come to terms with. When we doubt our worth, He compels our spirit to press and push on. He ordains and He formulates the mission ensuring that we are able to bear the circumstances and bring forth the fruit of His grace and love. He continued to keep me in His embrace, and under the auspices of His mercy. For that, I am so thankful and grateful. Jesus' ministry didn't go without challenges. The patriarchs before us ministries didn't go without challenges and the majority of them became martyrs for the Lord's will and purpose. Is it possible for us to obtain such a relationship and commitment with the Father, Jehovah?

I can't begin to tell you when I started to unknowingly use my good Christian upbringing and mild decent manners as a tool for my propensity to live my sinful nature. **"OWN IT"** As I write about it now, I can tell all of you that we must possess the guidance of the Holy Spirit and make positive spiritual choices. From my debauchery and heresies, you can clearly see how good can be used for evil and destruction. If we can ask the question, is it too late, then the answer is no it isn't. Still the question how long does it take lingered over my life.

I was asked the question what are you doing to stop and put what you can on hold. I couldn't answer that question, because I continued to make a mess of things. I really needed to stay away from nothing ventured nothing gained. Ventures and gains were all of a focused calamity as it concerned me. During the harsh times after my third divorce, I stepped back into the church and began to testify and confess my sins first to the bible study group, The Fathers of St. John.

There were some strong deacons and brothers in the class that had been through somethings and had triumphed over the negative outcomes. With my brothers in Christ, I felt free from scrutiny and judgement in the bible study. I almost wanted to believe that there weren't any Christians in the study. They embraced me and encouraged me to just keep pressing and looking forward.

I had two yearnings in my life. One was being a better father to my children and the other was Daynay. Watching television one evening, I heard a woman call another woman "a childless whore." She was speaking to a woman that had children, but other people were nurturing, raising, and caring for them, while she spent her time whoring and sexing with other women's husbands. Daynay was my equivalent of a childless whore.

GOD KNOWS YOUR NAME!

Neither of the two yearnings would be easier than the other. When you've scared folks and abandoned them at their weakest hour, if they survive the moment or situation, they construct defenses that bar them from allowing any type of reoccurrence in any shape, form, or fashion to happen again. You can approach them with God, passionate apologies, clear and concise change, or tears filled with begging and no amount of chiseling will work. I started a fight with the mothers of my children using insufficient, poor rhetoric, and tone.

They had every intention on keeping the fight going until I either went away or heeded to their wishes. It felt like psychological warfare to me. I couldn't make any suggestions, or have any input on the nurturing, rearing, or raising of my children, because that would be construed as me trying to impose my will. When I had visitation with my children, they only saw, heard, and witnessed a father that loved them and taught them to love and serve God. Even though their mothers didn't think so, that was the truth. In the midst of the carnage, and child battles, I found a way to proclaim _right always wins_.

GOD KNOWS YOUR NAME!

Deuteronomy 6:4-9

[4] Hear, O Israel: The Lord our God is one Lord: [5] And thou shalt love the Lord thy God with all thine heart, and with all thy soul, and with all thy might. [6] And these words, which I command thee this day, shall be in thine heart: [7] And thou shalt teach them diligently unto thy children, and shalt talk of them when thou sittest in thine house, and when thou walkest by the way, and when thou liest down, and when thou risest up. [8] And thou shalt bind them for a sign upon thine hand, and they shall be as frontlets between thine eyes. [9] And thou shalt write them upon the posts of thy house, and on thy gates.

Right always wins is another statement of fact for me. You might remember earlier my other statement of fact was that nobody wins in a war and war changes a man. What is your statement, or statements of fact? We can't approach the Holy

Spirit with the desire for answers to questions that we ignorantly, or arrogantly fail to develop, or face. Did I really believe that right always wins, or was that a scapegoat moment that suited the covering of my transgressions? For me, *right always wins* was based on my focus, and character that dwelled in love and truth after I evaluated, and examined myself under the guise of the Holy Spirit. The possibility of change is real and attainable.

Psalm 139:22-24

[22] I hate them with perfect hatred: I count them mine enemies. [23] Search me, O God, and know my heart: try me, and know my thoughts: [24] And see if there be any wicked way in me, and lead me in the way everlasting.

Daynay, my sexual affair with a co-worker, was the catalyst that wouldn't allow me to stop living this **CHRISTIAN LIVING LIE**. This Jekyll and Hyde theme continued to tug back and forth at me. Here I am wounded, and scorned with very little support from anyone mainly because I couldn't show them who I had become before I arrived at now. Daynay had carnal knowledge and was a great instrument for Satan. She had this laid back, cool, and calmness about her that made me lavish in our sexual relationship, and it would leave me in a spiritual and flesh battle that I didn't have the tools, or the armor to end it.

For this type of behavior and sinful acts, my grandmothers would call us bastards. That nor depression, nor guilt, nor despair would prevent me from being with that woman. I tried to develop other relationships and spend more time with others going out to dinner, amusement parks, or social events, and nothing kept me away from her. This wasn't right and I wasn't winning. Weakness is a part of the question in life. Whether living it, facing it, or running from it, you will experience the devastation of it at some point in our lives.

I didn't need that big house anymore, so I sold it, and moved to an apartment on the next street over from where the house was located in Milton. The move from the house to the apartment went smooth without a hitch and the children and my yellow lab, Gizmo, adapted nicely as well. I was able to pay off some of my legal and credit debts and took a quick trip down to California to see my Uncle Jr. and Aunt Jean. That trip and visit always provided a breath of fresh air and renewed purpose. You'll be hard pressed to find anybody that put fire and heat to food like Aunt Jean, however; when we depart from an ongoing situation, the situation is still ongoing when we return, and is worse in most cases.

That's how I've come to know that leaving or running isn't the way to deal with issues that may be of grave consequence to others. To remain in an abusive, or harsh state of mind for an extended period of time is psychological calamity. The rhetoric and tone of my actions didn't help the situation at all. I developed a desire, and passion to figure some things out, so it was time to remove a domino to prevent the other dominoes from falling over. I couldn't quite see, or know what that was, but it would be made clearer to me soon. Observe what happens next, when goals are weak and unsound.

Tuckina, my high school girlfriend, came to Milton to stay with me for a while. She was having marital troubles and I was hovering in serious relationship lonely land, so why not see if maybe some of what we had as teenagers was real. She didn't know about Daynay, Malaysia, Baby Mama, Lawsuit, or Court Clerk. *That's loose cannon kind of stuff.* Taking life and the institution of marriage as if it were some kind of fishing trip, or smoke break is criminal and spiritual suicide.

We had better start giving our ignorance's the weight and condemnation that it deserves. We committed adultery of course and I know you were waiting to hear that, and maybe even some of the sloppy details, but I told you this ain't no romance novel, neither is it a smut magazine. This is me informing you about the hell that is waiting for you, if you don't answer the question in life, how long does it take, get your moral compass calibrated, and answer the call and assignment that God has for your living and life!

Just for the sake of a teaching moment, the adultery was committed when it entered my thoughts to get her phone number to call her. It's not okay to camouflage those thoughts with childlike innocence. If God could label us shmucks, do you think he would? No, we didn't have that forever love for each other, but something so amazing occurred while we were together in that apartment. She and her husband began to reconcile, and repair their marriage. Marvin, don't you even try to say, or take credit for any part of that by thinking that committing adultery with that man's wife was what their marriage needed to survive. What did happen was encouragement and the opportunity to discuss what God wanted out of the circumstances. It's funny how we can right the ship for others, but our journey is still un-navigational. They're still together in love with each other till this day!

GOD KNOWS YOUR NAME!

While still hovering in serious relationship lonely land and taking some time from the job, I immersed myself in playing with Gizmo, shouting, chess, golf and hanging out by the pool. It's okay to use worldly efforts to mask problems and issues, but the Holy Spirit contains the real and sufficient answers. Gizmo loved chasing after his ball and swimming. I would take him down to the waterfront, and throw his ball out into the lake as far as I could, and he would fly out into the water before the ball left my hand. That was the most peaceful and calmest time that I had ever experienced in my life. That's correct. Gizmo was peace for me. If life for me could remain being about him chasing his ball, peaceful bliss would remain forever.

To hear the waves and to see his tale waging so rapidly, was priceless. It allowed my thoughts to trace back to all of the beautiful parts of God's creation that I had been privileged to see and visit. Places like Cannon Beach Oregon, Maui Hawaii, The

Philippine Islands, Barcelona Spain and on and on. Anywhere on God's creation, that man hasn't defaced yet, is absolutely gorgeous. Just as I felt good and comfortable with loneliness, Daynay calls with an offer to take me to Joshua Tree National Park in California. Go if you ever get the chance.

Taking back, or trying to erase 34 - 37 years of harsh rhetoric, aimless actions, impulsive decisions and horrible living isn't possible with humans. Even with new relationships, or commitments several questions will be asked and need to be conclusively answered. I made the mistake of thinking and believing that if I just backtracked, and reached out to as many of the people that I could find that I sinned against and sinned with, that I could somehow turn the tide. My χριστιανός experience and walk with the Lord hadn't arrived just yet, but my **CHRISTIAN LIVING LIE** was going strong.

The first crucial blow that I received from that approach was from the mothers of my children, which happened to be a former girlfriend and an ex-wife. It went down like this; "you can stay over there with that spiritual, religious bullshit, because I know who you are." I found that difficult to understand, because at the time I didn't know who

I was! But now! But now! That was the least of the responses and communications I received. For the majority of my efforts, the atmosphere was silent. The issue or wrong doing was insignificant, because they were dealing with other relationship issues. I didn't feel any better or very good about it, because I may have paved the way for others to invade and abuse.

What was worse is that because of me they weren't able to commit or trust. Be true to the creature that God made, that is the only way you prevent dragging others through the mud, and spiritually ensure that your heart and house is clean. I did it in the reverse order, and I paid a heavy price for my flawed character. The accusation for those that parlayed with me is complicit, but who gets and accepts the rebuking from the Lord? Who stands in the path of righteousness for His name's sake when others get to enjoy the masquerade?

Psalm 23:3
He restoreth my soul: he leadeth me in the paths of righteousness for his name's sake.

GOD KNOWS YOUR NAME!

Chapter 19: Growth Speaks Vividly

Prior to my third marriage, I had elevated my church and bible study attendance. In addition to the Fathers of St. John on Thursday nights, I also went to the Tuesday night lesson that was taught by the Pastor. The way he navigated through the scripture and lined it up with life and living was awesome. Now I know and understand that he was articulating, and transferring the Word of God from the Then and There to the Here and Now.

My prayer regiment changed and my spirit had begun to find some peace and solace from the lawsuit, divorces, visitation and parenting differences, and so on. I actually put my eyes on scripture in my home, and not because I went to a bible study. God's Word, the bible, seemed to be more searing from a different perspective in my private study. The quiet, the focus, and the cognitive search for me and my transgressions in the scripture would start to convict and encompass my behavior and desires. **Take a deep breath.** I prayed for the Lord's guiding hand and touch to do what I couldn't possibly do. The Pastor told me, "It's a waiting game and you're in a holding pattern.

We're all put in a holding pattern at the airport before we lift off and before we land."

He pastored over 4,500 members and he made time to tell and teach me that. He always made time for the betterment of people. The church and Pastors around here have some catching up to do. The church is in a fragmented culture at the moment and in need of a collaborative measure to create unanimity in Christ. This will take some doing and prayer, but it's a passionate topic for me, so we'll see what transpires in the future.

When you pray for something, be specific and precise. God doesn't deal in ambiguity or confusion. I asked the Lord to sustain me when I returned to work. What exactly does that mean? I can't answer that now, so forget about 22 years ago. I returned to work after my short stint for a reboot. I begin to notice that I had a heightened response to some of the basic inmate issues. That's something new and I couldn't see where that was going or how it would play out. Then I began to oversleep and come close to being late for duty.

Daynay amped up her sexual attention toward me and I would basically have a 10 - 15 minute nap before I headed back to work. Add some part-time sex with Baby Mama, Malaysia, the lawsuit widow, and a Court Clerk to the equation and watch the fall out. How could I expect the Lord to sustain me in anything, if I consistently did all that I could to tear myself down? Maturity hadn't been achieved. Living in the carnal state hadn't been eradicated nor prayed over to life in a spiritual state.

My fellow officers started to notice that I was becoming unapproachable. That may have been on purpose, but the thing is that the inmates started to notice it as well. Remember my PTSD and Gulf War Syndrome; you're getting a glimpse at some of it. When we fail to address the issues of life, they don't just disappear. They linger and form a toxic decay with the stench preceding it allowing Satan to have the last laugh. A two month stay at the VA Medical Center in Mississippi addressed my PTSD issues. Why are we so afraid of tried-and-true methods and solutions? Why are we so afraid of giving testimonies and confessions? The answers are accountability and vulnerability. Take an extended crucial amount of time examining that supposition. This is also abandoning the truth.

While on duty at my post in the lobby of the jail in downtown Seattle, suddenly I could see thru the glass doors from across the street a bump in the concrete. It moved from across the street and came through the courtyard and under the glass doors then under my staff station causing me a small hop up. I turned and watch that bump go under a wall and disappear. I asked the people standing near me if they saw or felt that.

I turned to look out of the glass doors again and the concrete was rippling like water in a direction toward the jail. I began to scream earthquake everybody out of the building. 4.5 on the Richter scale. That 12-story building shook and rocked like it was made of rubber. The ground shuffled and shimmied. Objects that weighed hundreds of pounds bounced and moved. God is in control!!!!!!!!!!!! He's speaking and I pray that we're listening.

In my prayers for God to sustain me at work, I also prayed for peace and silence and for a wife that was just for me and me for her. My desire for her was to be a Christian with a relationship with God. Maybe I should've let God choose her as well. The woman that would eventually become my third wife came from Louisiana to visit me in Milton, Washington before I sold the house.

My mother lived with me at the time and they didn't have much love for each other. Other than the bump in the road with my mother, we started out great, but the mother issue kept coming up. My mother never had a word to say about anything dealing with my marriages. She stayed out of the issues in obedience to God's word. Before her, wife # 3's visit to Milton, we had more than a hand full of months of conversations on the phone as often as two or three times daily. We discussed the spiritual life and the carnal life at great lengths. So, what went wrong, you might ask?

To make it plain and simple me, I still possessed that I can easily walk away attitude with the lust and sexual relationships I still had with Daynay, Baby Mama, Lawsuit, and the Court Clerk as my slam the door on my way destinations. All my third wife had to do was express her dissatisfaction with an issue to give me the motivation to carry out my indulgences and propensities. Being married filled the loneliness void in my life, but love and sacrifice should've been my reason for marrying her. When you don't know yourself or unable to be real or true to the spirit, then you make those types of decisions and choices. So much suffering and backlash came from our union and subsequent divorce.

She had a relationship with God and she was raising her two children in the ways of the Lord.

They prayed, attended church, bible study, Sunday school and learned and recited scriptures on a daily basis. From the start, it was clear that our children didn't quite mesh together. My children had that laid back west coast attitude and rearing, while she has raised her children with that deep conviction to well manners and southern, corporal punishment. My children only saw fit to say yes sir, no sir, yes mam or no mam, to the elderly and her children said it with every response to a question.

GOD KNOWS YOUR NAME!

I was raised the way she was raising her children, but I had lived in a different culture and the geography and landscape of the topic had changed. I understood the method, but the dispensation had changed. She felt that my children would take away from what she had taught her children and my children had to act as hers, or they would suffer the southern wrath. We did all of the things that Christians do, but we were living a lie. The husband and wife never became one because I could never torment, brutalize, or physically scare my children. The lie, that we were living, will become clearer as I reveal more to you.

Clearly there's much more work to be done concerning me and my arrogance, stubbornness, infidelity, predatory habits and emotionally blind behavior. For what purpose was I living? Why are we quickened by The Holy Spirit? As I continued to engage in living and conversing about my path in life, someone said to me "something couldn't have been wrong with all of those women." Something was wrong with them, because they decided to enter into a relationship with me. I was a Christian that had consistent and normal Christian characteristics. Most of us function at certain levels of life, and I just happened to function at an irresponsible level for the majority of my adolescent and middle age life and that's not difficult to admit. *It's out there now for your healing, deliverance, and comfort.*

Indeed, we all have our issues, indulgences, and propensities, but my desire, mission, and hope are to focus on my issues and indulgences because the χριστιανός that writes to you about them now can show you the correct spiritual path to take and the correct spiritual choices to make. I'm not pursuing an avenue to make you feel deplorable or incapable. Pray for me as I pray for you. As a child, I didn't consider or imagine that I would enter into the cycles and situations of life in such a devastating manner not with the childhood and upbringing that Evelyn provided. Thank the Lord for His stabilizing force. He stabilizes my rhetoric and tone as I communicate and enunciate His love and word.

GOD KNOWS YOUR NAME!

Chapter 20: The Slaughtering Type

Every time I engaged in sexual intercourse and discussed sinful topics with Baby Mama, Lawsuit, Malaysia, Daynay, and Court Clerk, I knowingly fed flesh and ability. When I say ability, I mean that I engaged in it sometimes just because I could. Even when I was married to all of my ex-wives, I committed adultery because I could. It used to be so frivolous, that I would pound my chest and say yeah, I got it like that.

None of these women were women that just any man could have. To have a woman that any man could have didn't appeal to my curiosity nor my flesh. Besides, men and women alike do hunt to conquer and feel the power and authority in the act of sex. Well, maybe women hunt for the purposes of love. I'm just pouring me out at the moment.

If you're on the other end of this with an emotional deposit into that type of behavior, please prepare yourself for the worst gut-wrenching feeling that you can't take away, ignore or get past. I can honestly say that when it caught up with me, I was taken aback and astonished at the level of hurt, frustration, anger and resentment that had built up over the years and from several people.

It kills a spirit to have someone come up to you and say that they can't trust or love, because of what you've done to them. For example, how does a spirit recover from the arbitrary decision and action of uprooting a woman and her children, taking them thousands of miles away from the only security and home that they knew exposing them to adult, Christian behavior which was mimicking to say the least? The sooner you can answer that question the better, so you to don't mimic a man that loves God spiritually and truly trying to love and care for his family. We've got to be the real deal as followers of Christ that includes men, women, and families.

In my mid-thirties and I'm fornicating with 4 women that I'm rotating and juggling and I don't have a single obligation or commitment with or to any one of them. They accepted that like it was the best option on earth. Why is that? Was it self-esteem? Was it a great financial investment? Was it a moon walking sexual climax? What was it, because I know it wasn't my physical capability, content or commitment? They all had jobs, hobbies, beauty, and body. A couple of them had a child. My answer to the questions was as plain and simple as this.

I displayed and lived a character of one who cared, but the truth was that when life came to a certain point, you were on your own. With two of these women, that certain point never happened, so I was able to feed my propensity without intrusion. What do you want out of life, if its mediocrity, then you won't have to travel far to find it. If its security and balance, then be patient love God, thank our Lord and Savior, and wait for the Holy Spirit to lead you to it. So amazing, that's the proclamation of guidance and choice.

My third divorce put me in a terrible tail spin for all of the aeronautical folks out there. With PTSD and depression looming and hovering, I doubted God and my emotional state. After every divorce, I had to pick up the financial pieces and the monitory pieces to begin all over again. The task elevated the pressure, effort, cost and ability. A divorce that one party just wants to be rid of the other party and the time and living together hasn't amounted to much is a breeze, **but** when you begin to add children, houses, cars, property, accounts and furniture, it gets messy, personal and vicious.

Because of not praying, not confessing to the church and lacking a higher degree of commitment, I began to lose my way. In those previously mentioned issues, there should be strength and stability, so why or what has happened to me that is preventing me from the correct actions? Why had another 2 years of my life as a husband and father gone wrong? One answer could be that when we indulge and commit to part time Christians, they confuse, derail, delay, and deconstruct our efforts and focus. In our daily living, we must propel, and excel through life's menagerie of windfalls and pitfalls. We must understand that the Lord's precept and concept is as such; the rain falls on the just and the unjust.

Matthew 5:44-46

44 But I say unto you, Love your enemies, bless them that curse you, do good to them that hate you, and pray for them which despitefully use you, and persecute you; 45 That ye may be the children of your Father which is in heaven: for he maketh his sun to rise on the evil and on the good, and sendeth rain on the just and on the unjust. 46 For if ye love them which love you, what reward have ye? do not even the publicans the same?

I'm reminded of the song that says, "take me back take me back dear Lord." I needed something to change what I was feeling. I remember someone teaching that things change when you take the focus off of your issues and problems and focus on what you can do to help others with their issues and circumstances. With the prayers and blessing of the Pastor, I started a single men's group. We met every Monday evening in the cabana at the apartment complex where I lived. We fellowshipped, broke bread and studied the Word of God. On some occasions, we would go out to eat, bowling, or a movie maybe just to do something fun and to forge relationships. As men of the same stature and circumstances, we could study, share and talk freely. Our experiences as single men and single divorced, or widowed men varied. We discussed how we handled situations and problems and how the Word of God said to handle the situations and problems.

We stayed away from judging and characterizing. We raised funds, did functions and volunteered our time serving others and helping others when and where we could. We grew in number and we strengthened men to be men especially when it came to being χριστιανός men for God. We preached foundation, foundation, foundation. Our bible study focused on the sensitive topics and issues that single brothers experienced and the single sisters as well. We critically and emphatically focused on single fathers being a major part of their children's lives whenever possible and supported that mission with maximum effort.

My oldest son has been upset, disappointed, and angry with me for years. He has indicated that I abandoned him when he was 3 or 4 years old, and suddenly popped up when he was 5 years old telling him that I was his father. That is true and factual and a serious situation, because he is a man now. He is referring to a time that I began a relationship with my second wife. I was caught and captured in the moment and selfishness in my behavior and choice. My indulgences and propensities were with the new girlfriend that became my second wife, his mother, Daynay, Malaysia, Lawsuit, and Court Clerk.

GOD KNOWS YOUR NAME!

My affection and attention should've been inclusive and multi-functional, but **_"I failed as a father in that season."_** Our relationship is still being plagued from my actions in my mid-thirties. Life without a relationship with my children has been menacing at times, but after you've devoted 10 - 15 years of love and parenting since then, outside of

God what else can you do? God has to move us forward, if we allow him to do so. For now, my son needs to know that I love, care and pray for him. How long does it take ought to be the question that all of us should reject and denounce from existence, because getting to the answer is costly, taxing and sometimes impossible.

Divorce, religion, relationships, finances, bitterness, mistakes, anger, hate, sexual affairs, and geography have kept me away from my youngest biological son. After several years of court battles, lawyers and tenzzzzz of thousands of dollars spent on court cost and legal representation, I just couldn't fight or struggle with the issue anymore. When the end comes for us, we are left standing alone with only what we've managed to tarnish or polish to answer for. My heart, spirit and finances had lost the fight and struggle to just do right by my children. This is where a move of God led me to serving His people. Depart from the consuming of this world and project the grace and mercy of the Father, God.

With every disagreement or court demand, my spirit and mental capacity took severe hits. Gulf War Syndrome, PTSD and depression played a major role in my ability to carry on with what seemed to be a never-ending battle. Parenting, rearing and religion of my youngest son were a fight and a constant battle that bought us back and forth to court 2 or 3 times a year. Just to be clear and to let you know, I stopped fighting. The ex and her new husband finances were greater than mine, and I was financially, mentally, and emotionally drained. I had no fight left in me. If God says it'll be so, then it will. I'll just continue to love and pray for him and his brother.

After my third divorce, the church, single men's group, bible study and family lifted me up, but I had been clinging and holding on to that love that I could never have. She is different from any marriage, Daynay, European, Asian, white woman, island girl, court clerk and Sparkle. For years passed, I've caused her to live an adulterous life sneaking around and communicating with me. It would take more than a three day and night hide in a dark room to get past all of my plaguing indulgences. Yes, I closed myself in a dark room for three days and nights. It helped, but that spiritual action wasn't for the worldly issues. It was for my emotional and spiritual position.

I thank God for His guiding hand and loving touch. For if it wasn't for His command and forgiveness, the darkness of my path would surely have continued and I'm sure my pursuit of her wouldn't have stopped. The mysterious things and issues in life are so exciting and intriguing to us. We should be exonerated or removed from that position, because it damages our peculiar designation. Thank You Lord, for redemption and change, that makes us whole again.

I had an awesome work ethic. Even from my days as a 12-year-old paperboy. I constantly maintained a job or two in my adolescent years, but I didn't have the same work ethic in relationships. I listened to lectures by Pastor Ursula and Apostle Sylvester Murphy. Placing the focus on investment and maintenance in relationships, Pastor Ursula suggested that, "the investment in a relationship should reap a return." An investment return might come in the form of stopping a generational cycle of divorce, or early teen pregnancy. It relates to the something for nothing metaphor.

Apostle Sylvester offered that, "we should critically and spiritually consider all things regarding relationships before we enter that realm of life." He provided the illustration of the female Eagle dropping branches for the male Eagle to catch before it hits the ground. This is how she chooses the male that she is going to mate with. The premise being in a relationship, can you support or catch each other if or when tough times are present and spirits are falling.

I would offer that we create a relationship investment and maintenance list. As simple as it may seem, the list serves as a reminder of the investments that you should make at certain times and in certain circumstances. Pray over the investment and for the expected return on that investment. Maintenance is a fact of life. Anything or situation that operates extensively without maintenance, is guaranteed to breakdown or crumble. In the military, we did preventive maintenance. Preventive maintenance keeps us ahead of the enemy's attempts to fracture our relationships. "And for the love of Christ," establish our relationships with spiritual and cohesive balance. Form relationships with those that are in your weight class and put God in it. In our relationships, imperatively we must be the investment that God ordained us to be.

This has to be a fiction book. There's no way that one man could experience, create, suffer thru, and cause so much disaster and confusion in 22 years. The book isn't finished. When the foundation is weak or poorly established, whatever rest or depends on that foundation is sure to collapse, crumble, or disintegrate. No, I'm not placing or leaning on blame, but the truth must be told. How long does it take applies to this situation and part of life. While we were raised to know and love God, God wasn't our motive. Christians living the lie have motives that roam all over the feeding grounds of the world. The fiction is in our existence if we're not experiencing, creating, suffering, and causing for God. Let's proceed and move forward to more of the lie.

GOD KNOWS YOUR NAME!

Chapter 21: The Holy Ghost Visits

Lots of sayings and phrases exist to psychologically assist us in handling or making sense of our path as it exists in life:

It is what it is:
- Someday you eat the bear and someday the bear eats you
- What's good for the goose is good for the gander
- Fear is fear alone
- A delivered true dose of life's reality is life reality
- The monkey in the room
- It's hard but it's fair
- Can't see the trees for the forest
- A zebra can't change is strips
- Right always wins
- What you don't know won't hurt you
- Etc. etc.

What is missing from the list? I would venture to say the informative healing, and salvation power of the gospel. In addition to catchy and cute phrases, we must seek to develop a jargon and rhetoric of psalms and proverbs. That is where we find the spiritual assistance in making sense of our path in life. They co-exist and lean on each other, creating a balance that is needed for being made whole.

GOD KNOWS YOUR NAME!

Ephesians 1:12-14

[12] **That we should be to the praise of his glory, who first trusted in Christ.** [13] **In whom ye also trusted, after that ye heard the word of truth, the gospel of your salvation: in whom also after that ye believed, ye were sealed with that holy Spirit of promise,** [14] **Which is the earnest of our inheritance until the redemption of the purchased possession, unto the praise of his glory.**

Now single again, I didn't strike up any new relationships, or attempts to wu any more women to socialize with or be sexually active with. I became a bit more reserved and grounded in my actions and movements. It felt like I was in that holding pattern metaphor that Pastor had given to me in our recent talk. During this time, I was getting advice on careers that didn't involve hair holds, takedowns and non-lethal methods of subduing people. Catfish farming didn't seem like it would be a fit for me, but a Christian book store did sound like something that was manageable.

We're still working on that option, so we'll have to wait and see what becomes of the thought. In this span of time, rocking and reeling was my function and I needed space and nothing, so I closed my bedroom door and stayed in the dark and separated from others and responsibility for three days and nights. I can't tell you what or if anything that it solved or helped, but a pause for nothing while standing for God is crucial in the race.

After 2 years of probing, dissecting and analysis, it was determined that I couldn't effectively stop life to battle my PTSD and Gulf War Syndrome issues, so Dwight shut me down. With one phone call, I was relieved of duty and sent home. Gizmo was pleased to know and hear that, because that meant more trips to the lake and swimming for him. I had more time with my children and my stress level was reduced to rubble. My propensity to sin wasn't going anywhere thou. Propensity to sin stays with us, but we must engage in the smothering of it with all of the spiritual armor available to us.

I took this time and strengthened in study and in proclaiming Christ. Confession relieves the sting of what we hide and think we're hiding from God. If we can't control our indulgence or propensity to sin, we should still confess on a daily basis. We grow in wisdom and knowledge as we confess and I can't begin to tell you what your confession may do for those around you, but I'm writing this book of confession to help in any way that I can.

GOD KNOWS YOUR NAME!

This book is my confession on a massive scale put on display for the world to see and read for the bible, the Word of God, says to confess one to another. It also gives me another opportunity to apologize to those who were part of a living lie and that were subjected to an aimless existence. I'm not taking or accepting the full weight of these indulgences and propensities, because the majority of these acts that were committed involved adults that also need prayers and forgiveness. I'm confessing for my healing, and for my love in Christ.

Romans 10:8-10

[8] But what saith it? The word is nigh thee, even in thy mouth, and in thy heart: that is, the word of faith, which we preach; [9] That if thou shalt confess with thy mouth the Lord Jesus, and shalt believe in thine heart that God

hath raised him from the dead, thou shalt be saved. ¹⁰ For with the heart man believeth unto righteousness; and with the mouth confession is made unto salvation.

Confessing the Lord Jesus Christ is conjunctive with God's plan of salvation. My prayer and confession contain the hope that I've come to know the redemption and forgiveness of God. In this confession I've focused on me and me alone and not for selfish reasons. In my opinion, I was a natural Christian that lived out of control without the consideration of what God had instore for me. What good could come from that? My **CHRISTIAN LIVING LIE** was absent of fear and reverence for God. Just keep reading.

When I worked as a corrections officer, my life would be threatened every day and sometimes multiple times in a day. It became common place and even dismissible jargon on some occasions. One of the affairs that I had with a co-worker escalated into a fatal attraction. *This ain't reality TV, this is a verifiable threat on my life and the life of my family*. Your life being threatened by incarcerated men and women, no problem, but by someone that's targeting you and those around you is completely terrifying.

She had knowledge of where I lived, the car I drove, my contact information, where my children lived, who their mothers were and the cars they drove, what time I worked and what hobbies I enjoyed and where I would go to have leisure time. It became a fatal attraction over a span of time that we engaged in mutual events and outings. To my amazement and astonishment, I truly feared that woman. I had to inform the authorities of what was transpiring, because I thought that a day might come when I would have to kill her. Just keep living carefree with unintentional malice, a philanderer's life, I'm sure your fatal attraction will locate and designate you as the primary target.

I'm reminded of my cousin's, Clarence Dunbar Sr. thought saying, "that I'm only responsible for what I do", but I would like to add "what I do and cause" to that statement. We should be cognizant of our actions and the subsequent negative causes that follow. As a result of our Christian antics and behavior, there is fallout.

With a renewed purpose and spiritual focus, we achieve positive results without the mention of fallout. Don't be hard on yourself when the wisdom and knowledge of this becomes clearer to you. Continue praying, repenting, rebuking and desiring forgiveness in God's time, you'll receive it and in God's time you'll make great use of it. Imagine the day that you can be about your Father's business.

A distance was being created unbeknownst to my intuition and witness. My appetite and thirst were changing. My demeanor and swag were changing to prepare for positive results and solutions. Caring and sharing was becoming common place and I was making a sacrifice to meet people on common ground. Investing into others and allowing my spirit to intermingle with theirs, was a risk that I accepted and embraced. I made the choice to put an end to baby mama drama, because the madness had to stop.

Daynay was being considered for a real relationship and not just a stop on my way from the golf course, or a sex toy that was there for me to play with when I argued with my wife and left home for a few days. The court clerk got the same attention. She made it as far as meeting the children. She was only the second woman that garnered that distinction. When we choose God, Jesus, and The Holy Spirit, our worldly options become limited and you start to recognize that you're not as lonely as you thought you were.

When the Holy Ghost visited me, I could reflect back on my philandering conquest. It shined brightly on my darksome path. Can you imagine someone crying and basically crumbling at the sound of your voice. Wow, Lawsuit, Baby Mama, and Court Clerk didn't have a clue. Blindsided emotions and feelings are fragile by nature, and the level of the affliction is not truly unmasked, until the crying and crumbling begins.

The transgression and iniquity list postured long and damning in the beginning of this venture is now considerably shortened. When hope disappears and despair sets in, unfortunately; we delegate all of our focus to the list of transgressions and iniquities. In these moments of our existence, we have to find a way to exist in God.

In God, we can go down in the valley and have our "Shane come back" "Shane come back" utterance for the established justified life of salvation. Our transgressions against God and people are turned into praise and respect. Iniquity loses its capacity as detriment and succumbs to spiritual motives and prayer solutions. This is an oldie but goodie and still has relevance "take it all back"

A woman with spiritual strength and resolve is what's needed for a man of God. She has to possess that "I'm going through and I don't care what the rest of the world decides to do" attitude and commitment. Past choices for me were fragile, unfocused, ill equipped spiritually, and lacked stamina. God's stamina is greatly required when we deal with matters of the flesh and spirit. We can't just wing this exam. We must approach this with study, work, blood and tears.

In 39 years of the **CHRISTIAN LIVING LIE**, three divorces and chasing after the light complexion and long curly or stringy hair woman, only one came close to being that woman with spiritual strength and resolve. When you're in the foxholes and trenches of life with a God given command and authority, you don't need a help meet that's looking back remembering and talking about what David, Jimmy, Doug, Pookie and Marvin did to her.

Watching your children experience heart ache, instability, insecurity, and psychological pain because of your actions as an adult is difficult to deal with once you're done being full of yourself. The pain, wounds and scars remain long after we stand up praising God and proclaiming to be a born-again Christian with a clean slate. Not so fast Homie, you got stuff to deal with potna. Stuff like, being an absentee father. A father full of promises, but short on delivery or maybe you helped procreate the child and failed to claim or care for it. Whichever maybe the case, <u>we as fathers have to put in the work.</u>

I can tell you that it won't be easy, because the ones that knew you won't know what God has done for you or how He's changed you. They'll deny and denounce your maturity as a Christian, while protecting what they love most. Mothers generally don't give predators a second chance to harm or damage their children, so be ready for the uphill battle and be reminded that the children form their own defenses as well. If Marvin Jr. or Trenton never consider me as their father or daddy, I understand because God knows what He's doing and what's best for them. In my heart and spirit, I only have love, concern, and thanks for them!

Just a common and simple man's viewpoint and it's not designed to tell you what or how to do it, because every case is different with a different set of circumstances. Listen, whatever you do be careful, be real, be committed and be spiritual.

GOD KNOWS YOUR NAME!

Chapter 22: God's View of Family

Most of my marital time was spent with the never-ending desire to be right or free from wives' concerns. I was a great provider with all of the trimmings, but I lacked in love, affection and understanding. When you get a chance, ask a woman or serious woman of God what's more important to her. As long as she had a banging body, light complexion, long hair and curly hair, I was satisfied, so I felt that I being a provider and taking care of what was satisfying to me was enough. To all of the white knuckled hard heads out there listen up, the woman is made from a rib bone of man that covers and protects the heart. She needs her husband to carefully and skillfully protect the matters of her heart especially with the guidance of The Holy Spirit.

Genesis 2:21-23

21 And the Lord God caused a deep sleep to fall upon Adam, and he slept: and he took one of his ribs, and closed up the flesh instead thereof; **22** And the rib, which the Lord God had taken from man, made he a woman, and brought her unto the man. **23** And Adam said, This is

now bone of my bones, and flesh of my flesh: she shall be called Woman, because she was taken out of Man.

GOD KNOWS YOUR NAME!

Marrying her in obedience to God makes her bone of your bone and a crucial step in the preservation of God's family. This must be said: Preachers, Pastors, Apostles, Bishops, Justices of the peace or whatever your title maybe stop marrying anybody that ask you to without them displaying or proving some knowledge of God's purpose or commandments on marriage. My philandering craziness and provider rights were a menace to God's intention and view of family. They were never questioned or investigated by any of the afore mentioned ordained to perform marriages.

You are the link that authenticates the honor in a marriage, but y'all are chasing the money or financial gain instead of the ordained institution. How is a marriage strengthened when the Godly authentic link that marries them isn't cognizant of our Lord's precepts and concepts concerning marriage and family? I know that to be factual, because I married three times under those conditions and circumstances in Las Vegas,

Denmark and Opelousas. We, I and my ex-wives, just showed up with the cash and license and y'all did the marrying. God is not pleased!!! I will never ascend to the Holier Than Thou peak, but I will accept, appreciate and proclaim my development and growth in wisdom, patience and love for God. Pragmatically speaking, with so many years of ignorance and non-productive sinful living, I'm willing to declare that the mantle is in good hands because of the reformation.

I'm reminded of the song that speaks about the pressing, beating, and shaking. It took all of those to make manifest the true χριστιανός foundation. I beg of you, as the Apostle Paul did, to come to a turning point. Come to a point in life where all of the intersections connect, fit perfectly and lead to the love and worship of God. It's not *Holier Than Thou*, but it's catchy.

To hear someone accurately tell you about yourself can be partly demeaning, antagonizing, enlightening, uplifting and enhancing. Often the observations of others hit their mark or fragile target causing retaliation or denial. In the military, we would say "you have to find your true north." We fail to know our longitude and latitude in life, so we take the position of how could someone else possess such knowledge. In the opening pages of the writing, I posed life as a question. Do not faint or be weary in the faith of answering the question in life.

Galatians 6:9

And let us not be weary in well doing: for in due season we shall reap, if we faint not.

For instance; the moment I and Daynay committed our last sexual act, she said that I was "just a nice dog" and she said it calmly and with sincerity. We know what that means in the carnal sense and world, but what does that mean to a Christian? It means that I as a Christian had taken what is good and used it for horrible purposes while achieving negative outcomes, but you're witnessing a shift in thought process and focus.

I struggled with trying to construct a new way of living after being removed from my job as a corrections officer. Sleep still remained hard to come by and the nightmares still plagued me. I felt as a failure feels, but I clutched on to the fact that this is going somewhere. When and where will we find what's God's purpose in all that we offer and experience? I could say at the end of the rainbow, since we know that the rainbow is a reminder of God's promise to us and that He's the beginning and the end of the rainbow.

Reflection and recollection became powerfully instrumental in my spiritual life as I pursued the answers to when and where for God's purpose. Through those actions I found a hallmark within myself. Suddenly, I had the tools and weapons that allowed me to come to the realization that all of this isn't me. My spirit said "fix it". From God's view of family, I flopped on more than one occasion, but by the renewing of mind and spirit change had come.

We can't go back and undo the **CHRISTIAN LIVING LIES**, but the quickening Holy Spirit can bring us back to living, a χριστιανός's fruitful living in which we seek and garner the love, grace and mercy of God. Living is likened unto a race and battle. In living, we must be Olympians and Soldiers for the purposes of God. The strength and conditioning needed can be found in The Holy Spirit.

The Holy Spirit gives us the choices that produce positive and advantageous results. It must be repeated that choice is more powerful than we think or know. We can expect God to do wonders and work miracles in our lives if our choice is to love Him through Jesus and obeying the Holy Spirit. His view of family and His plan of Salvation rest on our capability to understand that precept and concept. His grace, love, and mercy are all aimed at rendering His people, His family every opportunity to make the Holy and Heavenly choices.

1 John 5:11-12

[11] And this is the record, that God hath given to us eternal life, and this life is in his Son. [12] He that hath the Son hath life; and he that hath not the Son of God hath not life.

Bridges were being built for an anointed passage from Christian to χριστιανός. The correct choice in design had to be realized before construction could start. An eye and spirit opening experience is necessary for the optimum design utilized for the bridge's construction. The main focal point of the bridge's success is the anointed passage that will lead us away from the **CHRISTIAN LIVING LIE** and unto God for our salvation. Seek reproductive support from other χριστιανόςs in the challenge of developing the optimum design.

GOD KNOWS YOUR NAME!

Nothing new is done under the sun, therefore; the older generation and the younger generation may have powerful input as reproductive support. Keep God first in your life as well. Pray for the countenance of the Lord to remain in you and on you. Be a reproductive χριστιανός that the Lord can work with. After making reflection and recollection part of the process, I focused on seeking forgiveness from God and those I wronged. His view of family wasn't represented in my **CHRISTIAN LIVING LIE**. I started a new foundation, not one that was perfect by any means, but one that sought the correct material and input. Choosing to change habits took me a long way. The force of habit is multiplied when it has power over choice.

Over the course of decades, it had become a habit of mine to talk nice, to treat with respect, to create a pleasant atmosphere, to be encouraging, to be a shoulder to lean on, to be a gentleman, and to be honest in my lack of dedication to anyone or anything. Reflection and recollection caused me to know that my habits were meritless of God's love and grace. We must fix it by making the necessary adjustments. The choice is ours. Praying, reading and studying the bible, rendering assistance, attending and participating in the church and connecting with God's people, brought a hallow change to my spirit. I made a great choice.

Chapter 23: The Thanks and Trials

At this point I must thank 2 professionals that assisted, supported and defended me in my personal trials, tribulations and life mishaps. Dr. Dwight Randolph and Attorney Kimberly April were the links in the chain that were missing for me. They squelched thoughts of hurting myself and others, especially when others were trying to hurt or take advantage of my situation. They successfully kept me above the fray even though my vain existence made it an uphill battle in the courts and healthcare system.

I had mentioned Dr. Dwight earlier, but that mention was only a minut portion of how thorough and intelligent he truly is. Attorney Kimberly always made me focus on being patient and letting the courts make its fair judgements. She kept me grounded and level headed through all of the false accusations and financial threats. What y'all said, advised, suggested, taught and recommended, prevented suffering and pain on a plethora of levels and issues. Thank both of you so much, because *you were the epitome of right always wins.*

PTSD, divorces, unwedded children, adultery, and strife are not burdens, but they are conditions in which life exist. The focus isn't on reliving or undoing 34 - 38 years, but to share knowledge and understanding of those years to prevent or help others get through those issues. This hallowing change is welcomed and received without question or hesitation. It's been a longtime coming.

When God makes us whole again, it doesn't look perfect not as in the end times. Time isn't complete yet, so we must be in the now. Now is the time to shower others with love and understanding. Develop a theme and routine that improves upon what God has done in the realm of hallowing your spirit and actions. Take advantage of the justified route to sanctification that He is affording you. We dismiss or ignore too many opportunities in life that are offered by the spirit that also go unattended because our visceral tendencies are flawed.

Give God the spiritual rock that He wants to build on. Being made whole isn't the flesh's time to be silent, to the contrary, it's time for a gospel explosion. You've been given an opportunity to see again with spiritual eyes. Our flesh needs to display a crazy, radical, functional praise under the auspices of the Holy Spirit.

Mark 10:51-52

⁵¹ And Jesus answered and said unto him, **What wilt thou that I should do unto thee?** The blind man said unto him, Lord, that I might receive my sight. ⁵² And Jesus said unto him, **Go thy way; thy faith hath made thee whole.** And immediately he received his sight, and followed Jesus in the way.

The Holy Spirit deserves a vigorous unimpeded praise that implodes seat placement and tares down generational differences and educational barriers. I would say become radical χριστιανός for the Lord.

Time being complete is better understood if spoken in the fulness of time. It had to be in the fulness of time that I was able to speak the undeniable truth about my predicament, promiscuity, vain existence, philandering nature, marital ignorance, parental deficiency, and indulgent behavior. With God's purpose spiritually engineered and implanted, the writing and teaching has begun. In the fulness of time, God's time, pertains to all that we are, all that we do, all that we'll become, and finally all that we'll end on.

Galatians 4:3-5

³ Even so we, when we were children, were in bondage under the elements of the world ⁴ But when the fulness of the time was come, God sent forth his Son, made of a woman, made under the law, ⁵ To redeem them that were under the law, that we might receive the adoption of sons.

Brother Clarence Dunbar Sr. often reminded a group of Laymen that the primary goal of our living should be arriving at in the fulness of time repented and unblemished. It's imperative, wise, pleasing, mandatory, and crucial to our salvation that we become knowledgeable, cognizant and dedicated to IN THE FULNESS OF TIME.

Mark 1:14-15

¹⁴ Now after that John was put in prison, Jesus came into Galilee, preaching the gospel of the kingdom of God, ¹⁵ And saying, **The time is fulfilled, and the kingdom of God is at hand: repent ye, and believe the gospel.**

Ephesians 1:9-14

⁹ Having made known unto us the mystery of his will, according to his good pleasure which he hath purposed in himself: ¹⁰ That in the dispensation of the fulness of

times he might gather together in one all things in Christ, both which are in heaven, and which are on earth; even in him: **¹¹** In whom also we have obtained an inheritance, being predestinated according to the purpose of him who worketh all things after the counsel of his own will: **¹²** That we should be to the praise of his glory, who first trusted in Christ. **¹³** In whom ye also trusted, after that ye heard the word of truth, the gospel of your salvation: in whom also after that ye believed, ye were sealed with that holy Spirit of promise, **¹⁴** Which is the earnest of our inheritance until the redemption of the purchased possession, unto the praise of his glory.

In the fulness of time contains the answers that we look for in incorruptible, immortal, twinkling of an eye, trumpet sounding, sting and victory. Without any doubt or hesitation, the χριστιανός is chumping at the bit for that moment in time. This notion of deliverance eases our trials and supports the well doing.

1 Corinthians 15:54-56
⁵⁴ So when this corruptible shall have put on incorruption, and this mortal shall have put on immortality, then shall be brought to pass the saying that is written, Death is swallowed up in victory. **⁵⁵** O death, where is thy sting? O

grave, where is thy victory? **⁵⁶ The sting of death is sin; and the strength of sin is the law.**

In the fulness of time is the χριστιανός's spiritual quilt. The ultimate cover, culmination and triumph over the peaks and valleys of life and the trepidation that plagued us as we struggled with our association with evil.

As you have been privy to my revealing of the <u>**CHRISTIAN LIVING LIE**</u> and trials, you may have formulated an opinion that may lead to questions of ambiguity. These questions are there to hinder and distort. You must know what purpose those questions serve, or you'll continue to <u>see what was and fail to see what is.</u> What is has its availability on blast for all of us if we can get pass flesh and self-distain.

I found it profoundly difficult to give my spirit credit for the seemingly small victories that the Lord placed before me. **I had questions instead of jubilee.** Because I had questions, it opened the door for Satan's devils to question, ridicule and doubt my spiritual journey. Too much of our relationship with the Lord is based on faith and trust, therefore; we must have the faith and patience that can't be measured or orchestrated.

GOD KNOWS YOUR NAME!

I met with the Pastor shortly after my declaration to preach the gospel. He skillfully and carefully acknowledged my spiritual position. He encouraged me to just be patient and he thought of us as diamonds in the rough. He formulated a plan and approach to get me where I needed to be in bible knowledge and church functioning. It started with me sitting on the front row. Then I and the three other people that accepted their calling, began taking classes to help us understand what was happening and to clarify what we wanted to do in ministry. The classes also ensured that our focus and ministry were Christ esteem and not self-esteem!

Attending a Seminary and Bible College was next on the agenda and plan. At the push and support of those around me, that action was achieved. It's a great accomplishment to get the milk and meat of the Word, but to get the foundation and spirit of the Word is awesome and revitalizing. Let me reiterate the power of choice. I chose to attend United Theological Seminary and Bible College in Monroe, Louisiana to solidify my calling in the sight of the saints of God and now I must do the work to walk worthy in Christ. Thanks, are in order for all of you that planted for God to water.

Ephesians 4:1-3

I therefore, the prisoner of the Lord, beseech you that ye walk worthy of the vocation wherewith ye are called, [2] With all lowliness and meekness, with longsuffering, forbearing one another in love; [3] Endeavouring to keep the unity of the Spirit in the bond of peace.

Chapter 24: Assignments Can Change

Retrofitted for praise, worship and duty, I jumped right in and began teaching a few Sunday school classes. Teaching wasn't new to me, because I attended two military schools that trained me how to teach, and I taught hundreds of classes during my 10 years in the military. I received a few looks of concern and that was quite understandable because I had taken ownership of my faults, disregards, babblings, and disasters. My recent divorce had played out for all of the church to see, so a concerned look was merited. My χριστιανός living example was in doubt of the people, but I bear strong and visible witness to the palm retentive attention and affection of my God!!!

John 10:28- 30
28 And I give unto them eternal life; and they shall never perish, neither shall any man pluck them out of my hand. 29 My Father, which gave them me, is greater than all; and no man is able to pluck them out of my Father's hand. 30 I and my Father are one.

How do you go from lying on your ex-wife and having her arrested to teaching a Sunday school lesson was a question that intended to hinder and hamper?

Romans 1:24, 28

24 Wherefore God also gave them up to uncleanness through the lusts of their own hearts, to dishonour their own bodies between themselves:

28 And even as they did not like to retain God in their knowledge, God gave them over to a reprobate mind, to do those things which are not convenient;

His grace is sufficient but His mercy is a necessity! To teach and receive God's Word requires the Holy Spirit, prayer, research, study, dedication, presence, facts and format. Not to be taken lightly, the teaching of the Word carries a huge demand to be spiritual and knowledgeable. The salvation of souls is the focus and concern. The Word of God speaks to us with the precision, patience, and power of an antidote for spiritual illness.

As I began to develop a more faithful regiment of prayerful thanksgiving and sustaining will for carving out a χριστιανός living for God, a different call or summons was made during this time. The call that I had prepared to receive all of my life it would seem. I answered the telephone and my mother's best friend, part of the village that raised me, said "Marvin it's time for you to come home baby. Your mother is sick and in the hospital." It was as if I had waited 23 years for that phone call.

Exodus 20:11-13

[11] For in six days the Lord made heaven and earth, the sea, and all that in them is, and rested the seventh day: wherefore the Lord blessed the sabbath day, and hallowed it. [12] Honour thy father and thy mother: that thy days may be long upon the land which the Lord thy God giveth thee. [13] Thou shalt not kill.

I had returned to the house of the Lord just as she raised and taught me to do. I wasn't restricted or pent down by employment or commitments. I didn't have any major issues that precluded me from hopping on a plane and going to Louisiana to be with my mother. **God Steppin In**.

My mother had a lengthy stay in the hospital. They couldn't figure out what was causing her to have so much pain and making her so sick. She was bed ridden for so long that she forgot how to walk. They sent her to a rehab facility for her recovery from the surgery that they performed. That four months stay yielded no progress. At this point, a decision had to be made. Place mama in a nursing home or relocate to Louisiana and care for her at 113 C. Alley.

The latter of the two seemed more appropriate to me, because I had witnessed all my mother had given and sacrificed for me and my brothers growing up. I made the move from Washington, the place I called home for 17 years, to Louisiana and I cared for my mother. It wasn't just the honorable thing to do it was the biblically responsible thing to do as well. It demonstrated my assignment as a χριστιανός and a son.

1 Timothy 5:2-4
² The elder women as mothers; the younger as sisters, with all purity. ³ Honour widows that are widows indeed. ⁴ But if any widow have children or nephews, let them learn first to shew piety at home, and to requite their parents: for that is good and acceptable before God.

I made a few more trips back to Washington to close up some loose ends and to say bye to my sons. I explained to them what was going on and why I was leaving, but they seemed not to understand the gravity of the situation. Our relationship suffered from the move, but I wouldn't change a thing when it came to taking care of my mother. God knows my heart and spirit.

I pray for them and for the Holy Spirit to give them the understanding that they need to get through life's barrage of ups and downs. In a court ordered parenting class, they warned and instructed parents not to use the children as pawns in adult disagreements. We have to leave certain issues and circumstances in the hands of The Father. Let's dig a little deeper.

While the task of caring for my mother was enormous, it didn't dampen my spirit and thirst to serve God and excel in ministry. I returned to the church where my spiritual roots were planted. Pastor Joel S. Greene Sr. observed me and licensed me as a minister. Later he moved the church to have an ordination service that gave me full authorization to perform all rights and honors as an ordained minister acknowledged by the State of Louisiana. I grew tremendously under Pastor Greene's tutelage and I thank him for all that he did to open pathways for me to serve God. It would be wonderful if I could end the testimony at this point, but the revealing of the **CHRISTIAN LIVING LIE** isn't complete.

Trips back to Washington led to chapters in life closing. Daynay, Malaysia, Court Clerk and Baby Mama were told goodbye. As I began to commit my final acts of flesh feeding with these women, I suddenly realize that I had lived most of my adult life in the darkness of sin and shameful indulgences. So dark and shameful, that I couldn't reveal it until now. You've been captivated by the sex and smut information and you've forgotten about the stealing, gambling, fighting, lying, suicidal thoughts, brushes with death and depression, etc. The light of the Lord is revealing the magnitude of the transgression, iniquity and calamity list.

Only now, I can inform you of the subdued impact of that insane list of deadly motives and actions. By deadly, I'm speaking of eternal death, hell. For so many years, my propensity to dwell in darkness wreaked havoc on my ability to return to the church. All it really took was for me to tell Satan, that suckka, I'm flipping the script and that I've got God on my side. The power of choice is so remarkable, but we continue to make the wrong and damning choices.

In the first few years of my return to Opelousas, I engaged in relationships with a couple of women, but none of them lasted. My "picker was off" as the millionaire match maker would say. Seriously, Satan threw curve balls at me when it came to me and having a dedicated monogamous relationship with a woman. Patience and trying by the firer are what I needed to incorporate in my relationship endeavors. The answer from The Holy Spirit won't come if you're not willing to wait, for example; I didn't date or talk to a woman about dating for 18 months. The χριστιανός path must be chosen when we approach this part of life because it's dealing with God's plan for the oneness of a man and a woman.

When I finally noticed a woman, it was her spirit that I noticed first. I would interact with her daily for brief moments and I invited her to attend bible study that we were conducting at home. Later, I noticed that my spirit wanted to know more about her spirit and this was a welcomed and drastic change from past indulgent behavior. I made a sign on a piece of paper begging her to let me take her out to dinner and I wore that sign for 2 weeks until she said yes. As a χριστιανός *not in a* **CHRISTIAN**

LIVING LIE at the age of 45, I married Laura a virtuous woman that loves the Lord more than she loves me!!! We've been married now for 11 years. Just wait and watch, what the Holy Spirit can do.

If I had met you sooner or earlier in life, is a statement that is often made after we have arrived at a grounded or rooted space in life. When I considered making that statement, I came to the conclusion and knowledge of this fact: If I would have met Laura sooner or earlier in life, I would've philandered, cheated, and committed adultery on her just as I did with the other women that I married.

The focus on the issue should be on the word **if**, because the existence of **if** is a strangle hold that we're keeping on our vision for the future with our current possibilities and successes. The word **if** will promote and sustain the willingness to constantly look back, be setback and not look forward. **If** is a beating and suppressing thought that encompasses mar and doubt. Don't get stuck on **if** and focus on **when**. The image, focus and existence of **when**, is where the spiritual trinity of life will meet you.

Sinning in the carnal life does not end, but I didn't want the moniker of sinner. We have to mix and match several different approaches and techniques to address sin while developing a new foundation for life. We know that it's a complex situation, because God labeled Lucifer as cunning and a snake. I heard a preacher refer to Satan as a suckka. Lucifer being his heavenly name, Satan being his earthly name with a world of devils working for him, therefore; we must start building with God.

To remain sinless is virtually impossible, but to remove sinful options and reputations are an awesome start. Some of us have already been introduced to God and a Godly living, so we have to return to our roots. Others may have to go through the acquisition process by way of lumps and bruises, before the making and molding by God can begin.

Proverbs 22:5-7

5 Thorns and snares are in the way of the froward: he that doth keep his soul shall be far from them. 6 Train up a child in the way he should go: and when he is old, he will not depart from it. 7 The rich ruleth over the poor, and the borrower is servant to the lender.

When we think that we have risen above and left behind our faulty history and faulty character, we might need to think again. I was informed by a woman from a previous relationship that I had a 16-year-old son. I tried to get him to do a DNA, blood test, to determine if that was indeed the fact. That situation, marrying a part time Christian, assuming the church going Sunday worshiper is saved and many other issues are all created and perfected by our faulty history and faulty character. All of which was brought to fruition due in part if not whole by my vain existence, impulsive decisions and poor choices.

All of these issues and circumstances share three common bonds: spiritually blind, spiritually deaf, and ignorance of God's assignment:
1) People can't see that God is the foundation by which you live on and the walk that you undertake now. **2)** They don't hear reverence for Christ and the knowledge and wisdom of the Holy Spirit in your confession. **3)** They don't understand your position or calmness and the countenance of God being on your life because they don't know Him like that. Still the question remains, how long does it take.

GOD KNOWS YOUR NAME!

For me, just about 38 years of my **CHRISTIAN LIVING LIE** had occurred. It has been a tumultuous time filled with sinful propensities, selfish indulgences, brushes with death, philandering, divorces, promiscuous behavior, career ending decisions, alcohol and drugs, STD's, neglect, unwedded children, PTSD and so much more catastrophic Christian behavior. Up to this point, I have restarted my adult path in life approximately five times. Five times after loving, working, creating, investing and nurturing I have promulgated dysfunctional outcomes. All of this transpired before the question was answered.

How long does it take? How long does it take for a child to overcome growing up without a father and to find **The Father**? How long does it for man or woman to stop their menacing behavior at the expense of other's well-being? Finding **The Father** is the premise on which I have shared the muck and mud, that I have gone through and put others through as they believed me to be a wholesome Christian and a decent person. Nothing was more rewarding in this plight of mine than the favor of God and my choice!!! I minister to several folks that miss this one fact; <u>they can choose for their issues and problems to stop.</u>

While I did careless, reckless, and carnal things in my **CHRISTIAN LIVING LIE**, God did the loving and spiritual things to see me through. Finding The Father erased faulty history and faulty character with a broad stroke and it was done suddenly and catapulted by choice. He, The Father, provided His son, Jesus, as an example and ransom and makes available the guiding Holy Spirit to shape our choices.

In my revealing and sharing, you're not going to know about the enormous and countless amounts of calamity, iniquity, transgression and immoral acts that I have committed, witnessed and observed being committed and suffered by others all around the world from state to state, ocean to ocean, continent to continent and city to city. You won't find much about my brother that died in prison, the brother that committed suicide or the brother that died from a crack overdose. You will not hear much about the mother that had to watch and suffer through the pain and agony of their plights, and the cloud and distance existing over and between my fathers' other children from a previous marriage and the ones born out of wedlock. My mother was eighty-five years old and still suffered from depression over the deaths of her children.

So much more could've been revealed, but I'm not creating a soap opera. Clearly, you can ascertain that iniquity and transgression has no limit. You understand that we cannot live the bastard's life, the Christian's life, for it is filled with demoralizing and decapitating behavior. **Please go from Christian to χριστιανός for the betterment and prosperity of our souls!** I just wanted to briefly shed some light on the subject, so you can clearly see the dysfunction and family's foundational weaknesses. We must work diligently and strive to preserve the institution of family, God's family. I began my spiritual and diligent efforts for the preservation of family by marrying a woman that loves God more than she loves me!!! With God centered motives and actions, visceral attempts at achieving His glory are secure and attainable.

For so many years, God steppin in has made me rich in a plethora of ways, but I wouldn't give what was required. If we continue, on this bastard's path of living our souls shall be required. The thought of this in a visceral sense should spark the rejection of certain actions in our daily living. Just read Hebrews chapter 12 for the knowledge of avoiding such a faith.

Luke 12:19-21
[19] And I will say to my soul, Soul, thou hast much goods laid up for many years; take thine ease, eat, drink, and be merry. [20] But God said unto him, Thou fool, this night thy

soul shall be required of thee: then whose shall those things be, which thou hast provided? [21] So is he that layeth up treasure for himself, and is not rich toward God.

An old adage from way back says "every tub must stand on its own bottom". There isn't one day that I have awakened and intentionally had evil, malice or reckless intent in my heart or purpose. For 39 years, I tried to place the blame on a dead man. "Every tub must stand on its own bottom" has a meaning and a mandate that guides us to responsibility and productivity while departing from the greasy grace mentality.

We must ask ourselves, at what age does it become my blame or fault? In my case, that was about to happen, but first the distractions and intrusions had to be removed. The apologies, feeling sorry for myself, looking back, clinging to material things, putting self before God, and not worshiping in spirit and in truth had to be removed and casted onto the grace and mercy of God.

GOD KNOWS YOUR NAME!

Chapter 25: Answers are Necessary

You've read and noticed that I periodically asked the question how long does it take, and I specifically repeated guidance and choice, and I pointedly announced God steppin in. How long does it take was a question that I developed after I realized the impact and effect that missing my daddy had on me. It deals with the issues, problems and malfunctions for me as a man and the span of time that I ignored or didn't bother to ask the question.

Did I want to be a predator targeting the most confident and courageous women for sport or even worse? No, and I never used that impact or effect as an excuse for my behavior. To answer the question and to adjust and change my behavior, I just needed to consult The Holy Spirit with an imperative attitude. 39 years is the answer for me. Please understand that 39 years is the answer for my χριστιανός ability to eradicate sadness and sorrow of not having my daddy in my life. My vain existence however; was nothing less than pure evil. I was the devil's instrument. Now you know the answers. The χριστιανός must venture into reality with a spiritual awareness for the fulfilling quality of love and respect for God and then His people.

Lacie, Joseph, James, Marie, Donald, Roy Jr., Donald, Ronald, Reginald, Willie Lee, Lisa, my siblings that I know and can confirm, we needed answers to some questions, but I'm afraid death has robbed us from the depth of such knowledge. We were born into the jacked up, ill-stricken, belligerent, and carnal actions of our parents. They lived a **CHRISTIAN LIVING LIE** as well. When God declares our come to Jesus moment, we must face the horror in the answers of our darkest reality. We do not have to die or expire with such guilt and shame. I'm so glad and blessed that God allows the spirit to sleep and rest from its labor.

As I spoke with my sister, Lacie, about our father's deeds, the lies within, and the sting of unfortunate rejection, to gain increasing knowledge within truth, she shared a funny story with me. The story was that of a lie. She said like "When Tony killed ZieK."

In their younger days they had a pet Hog, **Tony**, and a pet racoon, **Ziek**. They returned home from church one Sunday and they found Ziek the pet racoon deceased. They asked our brother Willie Lee what happened and he said that Tony, the pet Hog, killed the pet racoon, Ziek. Tony and Ziek grew up from bottle fed infant pets to mature adult pets in that house, so they were left with the question, "Why would Tony kill Ziek?" With an added look at Ziek, the deceased pet racoon, it was evident that Tony, the pet Hog hadn't caused Ziek's fatal wounds, so our brother Willie Lee admitted that he returned home from hunting and when he came in the house Ziek, the pet racoon startled and scared him so he shot Ziek. She said Tony lived in sadness and misery because his friend Ziek was gone. Some answers are devastating, but we need them none-the-less.

Unbeknownst to us, we live lost with a vain existence arrogantly and ignorantly denying the need for a more suited (χριστιανός) way of living. We're burdened and saturated with misguided efforts because of our non-existent dialect with The Holy Spirit. Answers are frightening when it concerns our behavior and relationship with the Lord. This is normal because as I said earlier, Heaven and Hell are real choices solidified by the judgement of Jehovah!

The life and heavenly sabotaging choices that we're making are made in the absence of The Holy Spirit's guidance. With the guidance of The Holy

Spirit, we would have a greater appreciation for the times that promulgated the fruition of God steppin in. This is the spiritual phenomenon that changes situations, circumstances and outcomes in heavenly proportions. **God stepping in** should be our main prayer, because He always steps in with His awesome love and power for the salvation of His peculiar people.

John 14:25-27

[25] These things have I spoken unto you, being yet present with you. [26] But the Comforter, which is the Holy Ghost, whom the Father will send in my name, he shall teach you all things, and bring all things to your remembrance, whatsoever I have said unto you. [27] Peace I leave with you, my peace I give unto you: not as the world giveth, give I unto you. Let not your heart be troubled, neither let it be afraid.

God steppin in, guidance and choice, and how long does it take are all elements in the design of a χριστιανός: **1)** Our questions need answers. **2)** Our path needs light and leadership. **3)** Our heart needs healing and purpose. Don't go against your design, because it grieves The Holy Spirit, shuns

God and is thankless for Jesus. As I move on let me say this, we are to work in the name of the Lord. That was our original mandate. When we work in the name of The Lord, we work in obedience and we are blessed beyond measure. When considering beyond measure, think of such on a heavenly realm. God's hand is on you!!!

On a TV show for National Geographic, they showed how Black Bears fight and feud with Brown Bears. They'll fight to the death if and when they cross each other's path. The one time in a year that they put their difference aside is at the annual salmon run upstream to spawn. For the Brown and Black bears, that is fellowship and feeding time. Just as some of us enjoy caviar, they do to. Nearest anyone can tell, they don't associate with each other because of their color.

Are the bears the same as humans, or are we worse than bears? At least once a year they put aside vain focuses and they cohabitate for the sake of survival. As χριστιανόςs, we must be better than bears. The vain killing and destruction of God's family and children needs to cease. The killing and destruction aren't exclusive to man, because Satan has his say so in the matter. There's a lie being lived and the truth needs to come forth and eradicate the spiritual injustices. In the heart of a χριστιανός, it should eternally be fellowship and feeding time. Fellowship in love with our brothers and sisters and jointly feed and feast in the word of God. That wisdom and knowledge is all the answering that you'll ever need!

Just speaking from my position, I have been through a great deal of mis-doings, un-doings, what-doings and why-doings. I don't need that pointed out to me anymore. I need love and prayers from those of you that know the Lord and His Dominion, Majesty, Might and power. With the mantle that we are entrusted with, unity and strength will be needed to fulfill God's will. If we are truly χριστιανόςs that know Jesus in the pardon of our sins, then let us walk worthy as such.

GOD KNOWS YOUR NAME!

Acting as Black and Brown bears do for 364 ½ days out of the year is the illumination of an evil strangle hold on our spirits. The song writer said "let it rise." The only way to be freed from an evil strangle hold is to offer up self to God and rid ourselves of self-preservation.

Romans 12:1-3

I beseech you therefore, brethren, by the mercies of God, that ye present your bodies a living sacrifice, holy, acceptable unto God, which is your reasonable service. ² And be not conformed to this world: but be ye transformed by the renewing of your mind, that ye may prove what is that good, and acceptable, and perfect, will of God. ³ For I say, through the grace given unto me, to every man that is among you, not to think of himself more highly than he ought to think; but to think soberly, according as God hath dealt to every man the measure of faith.

With all that I've been through. With all that I've done. With all that I've been complicit in. With all that I've been carelessly apart of. With all that I've been supportive of in my bad and good, I want to say something as simple and common as humanly possible. Take advantage and make good use of the opportunities and chances that God gives you to live for right and good. Denounce and fight wrong and evil. Live in the joy of knowing that GOD KNOWS YOUR NAME!

God gave me more chances than I can count on both hands. What if **GOD** only gives you one chance? Through it all, **He kept me** from AIDS, Drug & Alcohol Addiction, Killed in Action, Prison sentence, Killed in Car Accident, Cancer, Killed in night club fight, Killed by wife or fatal attraction, and all manner of brushes with death. God did all of that. *Imagine how much more He can do with more for Him to work with.* Start with God and stop at salvation.

Again, this χριστιανός, a simple man, a common man that was raised by a village in the ways of the Lord now has only to offer The Truth, The Kerygma, The Logos, The Good News and The Word of God. Halleluiah ought to be shouted to the heavens for the fruition of this journey. No more neglect, shame, ignorance, depravity and disrespect of the church and the process evolving into an obedient and repentant child of God.

Romans 1:15-17

[15] So, as much as in me is, I am ready to preach the gospel to you that are at Rome also. [16] For I am not ashamed of the gospel of Christ: for it is the power of God unto salvation to every one that believeth; to the Jew first, and also to the Greek. [17] For therein is the righteousness of God revealed from faith to faith: as it is written, The just shall live by faith.

Chapter 26: The χριστιανός Lives

A 39-year journey of a **CHRISTIAN LIVING LIE** has been revealed. Loud from the mountain tops, it came true. The actions and decisions that made me so ingratiating is now **Christ centered, ordained by God and led by The Holy Spirit.** Now as a minister of the gospel at 58 years of age, and the very point in life that I prayed for you to be in on page 2, my focus is on daily repentance and the spiritual plight of the world.

As I've considered and reasoned the plight of the world, I've come to know that no matter how strong your spirit or soul tie is with the Lord, do not get too comfortable. God Himself was with Adam and EVE and the cunning serpent was able to beguile Eve and ultimately Adam.

Genesis 2:16-17, 3:1-6

[16] And the Lord God commanded the man, saying, Of every tree of the garden thou mayest freely eat: [17] But of the tree of the knowledge of good and evil, thou shalt not eat of it: for in the day that thou eatest thereof thou shalt surely die.

1 Now the serpent was more subtil than any beast of the field which the Lord God had made. And he said unto the woman, Yea, hath God said, Ye shall not eat of every tree of the garden? **2** And the woman said unto the serpent, We may eat of the fruit of the trees of the garden: **3** But of the fruit of the tree which is in the midst of the garden, God hath said, Ye shall not eat of it, neither shall ye touch it, lest ye die. **4** And the serpent said unto the woman, Ye shall not surely die: **5** For God doth know that in the day ye eat thereof, then your eyes shall be opened, and ye shall be as gods, knowing good and evil. **6** And when the woman saw that the tree was good for food, and that it was pleasant to the eyes, and a tree to be desired to make one wise, she took of the fruit thereof, and did eat, and gave also unto her husband with her; and he did eat.

You've come too far and worked for so long and a worldly setback of such magnitude can be avoided. Prayer, repentance and worship have brought us from a mighty long way and salvation is sustained by our commitment to remain prayerful, repentant and worshipful. The worldly people, situations, circumstances, decisions and living can interrupt and sneak in causing a worldly reaction and down spiraling affect that kills and destroys.

John 10:7-11

⁷ Then said Jesus unto them again, Verily, verily, I say unto you, I am the door of the sheep. ⁸ All that ever came before me are thieves and robbers: but the sheep did not hear them. ⁹ I am the door: by me if any man enter in, he shall be saved, and shall go in and out, and find pasture. ¹⁰ The thief cometh not, but for to steal, and to kill, and to destroy: I am come that they might have life, and that they might have it more abundantly. ¹¹ I am the good shepherd: the good shepherd giveth his life for the sheep.

GOD KNOWS YOUR NAME!

Seriously, spiritually guard your actions and responses with your spouses, friends, coworkers, peers, community and acquaintances. It's what we don't know or see that comes back to haunt us. We understand the difficulties in faith and truth, so we must be aware of the chameleon rhetoric and the living of those around us. We're very aware of the propensity to abandon the truth due to its discomforting and exposing power. Make every effort to understand the problem, so that you can be a productive part of the solution. Let's learn and examine life so we understand what is in the spirit and what is in the flesh. Just entertain all of humankind respectfully and adequately according to the Word of God.

I can't begin to explain the God ordained spirit filled joy that overtakes me when I think about being delivered from indulgences and propensities. God is looking and waiting to deliver and consecrate the scapegoat in all of us. He will remove past transgressions, iniquities and calamities from your path and sustain you in your spiritual endeavors. We just need to get out of our own way. At some point we have to get exhausted from tripping and hurting ourselves with the self-sustaining ways of the flesh. Get on board, you won't regret it.

I asked someone to preview this book and my writing and to offer me their honest assessment of the content and candor in the information. At the completion of their reading, they saw the sexual history and behavior and the scripture quotes, but not much was said about the transgression, iniquity and calamity in its entirety. After reading this book, if sexual tendencies are all that you've gleaned from the testimony and confession, please read it again because *you've missed the vital and spiritual lessons and teaching within*.

Apparently, it's horrific and traumatizing to engage in sexual complicity, but it's acceptable to engage in the acts that lead to sexual complicity. Stealing, drinking and drug usage without temperance, fighting, absence of love, no church affiliation, vain existence and even more was all ignored and less scrutinized. *Please, find the lessons and the teachings*. Abolish your vain existence and allow the χριστιανός in you to triumph for God!

I speak to you now with the same message that Jesus and John had for us, repent. In this revealing of my **CHRISTIAN LIVING LIE**, I pray beg, and hope, that you let this testimony and outpouring change your thoughts and focuses. Seek the guidance of The Holy Spirit and His assistance in your choices. *It's our choices that are so powerful and controlling*. They can denigrate or uplift. We have the option to suit ourselves. I'm aware that God tells us to be and know that He is The Lord, but that doesn't strip you of making the choice to praise and worship Him. The power is in your choice.

The Christian moniker is nice and toasty for the tyro and novelist, but the χριστιανός moniker should be the understanding of God's grace, love through His Son, and conversations of joy and peace with The Holy Spirit. We must push ourselves to abide in the limitless spirit of our Lord and Savior, Jesus Christ. He came as the only pure and righteous example in the Kingdom of God.

Remember my statements of fact: **1)** NOBODY WINS IN A WAR AND WAR CHANGES A MAN. **2)** RIGHT ALWAYS PREVAILS. If you are following God's plan of salvation, which is found in the gospel and in the blood of Jesus Christ, then you're encompassed by righteousness that always wins.

Luke 1:76-80

76 And thou, child, shalt be called the prophet of the Highest: for thou shalt go before the face of the Lord to prepare his ways; 77 To give knowledge of salvation unto his people by the remission of their sins, 78 Through the tender mercy of our God; whereby the dayspring from on high hath visited us, 79 To give light to them that sit in darkness and in the shadow of death, to guide our feet into the way of peace. 80 And the child grew, and waxed strong in spirit, and was in the deserts till the day of his shewing unto Israel.

It was right for me to inform you about my **CHRISTIAN LIVING LIE** in *From Christian to χριστιανός*. God is pleased with our ability to rise above persecution, condemnation, blame, arrogance and ignorance. He is also pleased in our ability and diligence to remain truthful and faithful. I have read David's prayer in Psalm 51 and I've prayed that prayer. **Psalm 51:10** is my anchor because it fits my spirit and my understanding of God's plan of salvation. In our wrong doings that others are doing wrong in complicity, we could only pray that they are able to pray, repent and please God as well. I bear strong and visible witness to the palm retentive attention and affection of my GOD.

GOD KNOWS YOUR NAME!

Thank you for your love, prayers and support. I pray that something you've read and discovered adds to your life and the lives that you'll share this with. All of my love and respect is given unto you !!! Just choose to be the χριστιανός that God desires you to be. He truly wants eternal life for all of us. Just accept His presence and His promises!!!

Chapter 27: Cumulative Thought

Please, if only one approach is taken, or lesson is learned, or method is adopted from my journey, let it be this:

Choose to act honorably and accordingly as it pertains to being a χριστιανός. Choose living clean and wholesome. Choose the gospel over profanity and vain babbling. Choose good over evil. Choose firm decision making over impulsive decision making. Choose the church over the night club and streets. Choose meaningful over irrelevant. Choose gain over profit. Finally, Choose spirit of the LORD before flesh.

The point is that it's our choice.

IN THE HEART OR CENTER OF THE BOOK, I DIDN'T MENTION MUCH ABOUT MY POSSESSION OF FALSE SENSITIVITY AND SHALLOW EMOTIONAL CONTENT THAT AIDED IN MY **CHRISTIAN LIVING LIE**. SENSITIVITY AND EMOTIONS ARE GOD GIVEN AND THEY PLAY A VITAL ROLE IN OUR FORMATIVE YEARS

AND WHAT WE'VE BECOME. NOW, KNOWING THIS SHOULD GIVE YOU CRITICAL INSIGHT TO WHAT CHRISTIANS THINK, SAY, AND BELIEVE!!! THE *CHRISTIAN LIVING LIE* HIDES BEHIND THE VICIOUS CHARACTER OF FALSE SENSITIVITY AND SHALLOW EMOTIONAL CONTENT.

I HAVE HEARD AND WITNESSED PEOPLE PROCLAIM THAT THEY'RE WAITING TO HEAR FROM THE LORD BEFORE THEY MOVE OR TAKE ACTION. THE LORD HAS PLACED A HEAD OF KNOWLEDGE AND WISDOM ON YOUR SHOLDERS AND NINETY PERCENT OF WHAT YOU CLAIM TO BE WAITING TO HEAR FROM GOD HAS ALREADY BEEN GIVEN FOR US TO MOVE AND ACT. MAKE A CHOICE AND DECISION THAT IN YOUR HEART YOU KNOW THAT THE LORD WOULD BE PLEASED.

LIVE FREE FROM THE **CHRISTIAN LIVING LIE** THAT I LIVED. IT WAS A CARNAGING OF PRECIOUS TIME THAT WOULD'VE BEEN MORE REWARDING IF I HAD COMMUNED WITH THE HOLY SPIRIT. I BEAR STRONG AND VISIBLE WITNESS OF THE PALM RETENTIVE ATTENTION AND AFFECTION OF MY GOD. KEEP GOD FIRST IN YOUR LIFE AND LET HIM AND HIS WORD COVER YOUR 12 AND 6, FROM THE GRACE OF GOD AND MY LOVE TO YOU!!!

44 YEARS IS ALL IT TOOK FOR ME TO MARRY THE WOMAN THAT LOVES GOD MORE THAN SHE LOVES ME. I DID IT WRONG 3 TIMES, BUT I NEVER GAVE UP ON GOD'S PLAN AND DESIGN FOR FAMILY. THE INSTITUTION OF FAMILY SIGNIFIES THE LOVE AND HARMONY IN ALL OF US AS ONE PEOPLE FOR GOD! WE MUST GRASP THIS CONCEPT WITH CRITICAL CONSIDERATION AND CONCERN. AGAPE' IS THE WAY TO REACH AND OBTAIN THE MEASURE OF HIS GRACE AND MERCY.

<u>THIS MUST BE SAID AGAIN:</u> THE THOUGHTS, CONVERSATIONS, AND ACTIONS, OF MEN AND WOMEN OFFER EXPLICIT AND IMPLICIT REALITIES THAT FRACTURE THE BEING, FABRIC, AND FIBER OF HUMANITY'S MOST PRECIOUS RESOURCES, LOVE and TRUST. AS THE LIVING BREATH OF GOD, WE MUST EXAMINE AND EXPLORE THE RECESSES IN OUR EXISTENCE BOTH SPIRITUAL AND PHYSICAL TO ELIMINATE RECKLESSNESS AND MALFEASANCE. WE BEING THE LIVING BREATH OF GOD, MUST FILL AND DEVELOP OUR RECESSES TO A MATURITY THAT EMBARKS, OR TRAVELS ON A SPIRITUAL FOUNDATION.

IN MY REVEALS AND ANSWERS, I COULDN'T BE FORTHCOMING WITH THE INDWELLABLE DETAILS BECAUSE I STILL HAVE TO LIVE IN THE

FACE OF UNRIGHTEOUS JUDGEMENT AND SCRUTINY. AS THOUGH WE ALL DO. THE ***CHRISTIAN LIVING LIE*** IS REAL AND TRUE. AS I LIVED IT, IT WAS BRUTAL, DEVASTATING, DETRIMENTAL, PALPABLE AND PIVOTAL IN MY RISE FROM EXTINCTION. BE AND LIVE THE NAME THAT GOD GAVE YOU. **COME AND ACHIEVE SPIRITUAL MATURITY WITH ME.** BE WHO'S YOU ARE NOW FOR WHO'S YOU ARE LATER!!!

THIS REVEALING OF MY ***CHRISTIAN LIVING LIE*** WOULDN'T HELP YOU OR BLESS YOU WITHOUT THE WISDOM FOUND IN THE FOLLOWING <u>PURPOSELY BROAD, QUESTIONS</u>:

1. Who are you? What are you? When are you? Where are you? Why are you? and How are you?

2. Why are we so troubled and scarred before we reach the age of 12 years?

3. What is the reason and purpose for the existence of us being a toddler to adolescent?

4. Who is responsible or held accountable for what we don't know?

5. What is our reward for receiving and cultivating the pleasures of others?

6. What goal or purpose is necessary for the totality of life?

7. Where does the use and abuse of anything made or created lead us?

8. Why would you get pregnant or make a baby with someone you've only known for a few weeks?

9. Do you know for sure and certainty that the foundation of what is to come is solid, firm, and rooted?

10. What is the route and path for tomorrow?

11. Who and what is accumulatively affected by our life?

12. How important is time and how much time is in a lifetime?

13. What is the nature and purpose for life's trouble, goal, pain, love, gain and fault?

14. Who or what profits from our bitter disputes, differences, and disagreements?

15. Where can we find the answers to the unexplainable facts and issues in life?

16. Does life and death mean anything?

17. What is the difference between gain and profit?

18. What is the real difference between good people and bad people?

19. Who should we trust with every detail and fiber of our existence?

20. What is the plan for everything in life?

21. Why does explainable and unexplainable matter?

22. Do you have any cares, concerns, or considerations?

23. Who are we as toddlers, young people, youth, adolescents, adults, and seniors?

THE ANSWERS TO THE QUESTIONS ARE GOING TO BE LIVED BY ALL OF US! I JUST WANTED TO PAINT A SMALL PICTURE AND TINY GLIMPSE OF THE VANITY IN LIFE. THE LORD PROVIDES ALL THAT WE NEED AND ANSWERS ALL THAT WE NEED. HE KNOWS OUR NAME AND WE SHOULD PRAY THAT HE BLESSES US TO LIVE UP TO THE NAME THAT **HE** HAS GIVEN US!!!

NOBODY WINS IN A WAR AND WAR CHANGES A MAN. RIGHT ALWAYS PREVAILS.

Love God, Thank Jesus and obey The Holy Spirit

GOD KNOWS YOUR NAME!
GOD KNOWS YOUR NAME!
GOD KNOWS YOUR NAME!

IF PROPHECIES, LANGUAGES, PHRASES, PROVERBS, OR CUSTOMARY SAYINGS ARE CONTAINED WITHIN THIS OUTPOURING THEY ARE NOT FROM A QUOTATION OR COPY FROM ANY OTHER AUTHORS BOOK OR WRITING.

GOD KNOWS YOUR NAME!

Special thanks to all of you whom our paths have crossed because God gets the glory from whatever we survived or shared in our time of knowing each other. Even if we were disobedient and contrary to the ways of the Lord, we ultimately forged a bond that saw us thru to this moment. In our mischief and despair or laughter and anger, we pressed on and found strength to make our outcomes livable and useful.

More thanks to those of you that have allowed and trusted me with leading and guiding you thru your career and future. Today to those of you that accept me as your spiritual leader and confidant, I say thank you.

To my Wife and family, you know that I love you and I gotchu !!!

GOD KNOWS YOUR NAME!

Appendix: Definitions

Χριστιανός : Greek *Etymology* (religion) Christian.

Adolescent: growing to manhood or womanhood; youthful.

Adorned: to make more pleasing, attractive, impressive, etc.;

Assailant: a person who attacks another, either physically or verbally: attacking; hostile.

Asterisk: A small starlike symbol (*), used in writing and printing as a reference mark or to indicate omission, doubtful matter, etc. Any factor or element that makes an otherwise outstanding achievement somewhat doubtful or less impressive:

Atrocity: Behavior or an action that is wicked or ruthless.

Bastard: Not a child of God. A person born of unmarried parents; A vicious, despicable, or thoroughly disliked person: Not genuine; False: Fake, Imitation, Imperfect, Sham, Irregular, Phony. Anything unpleasant or arduous;

Beguiled: To charm or divert: Influence by slyness.

Beleaguered: To trouble persistently; Harass.

Calamity: A disaster or misfortune, especially one causing extreme havoc, distress, or misery.

Callous: Insensitive; Indifferent; Unsympathetic. Made hard; Hardened.

Candor: The state or quality of being frank, open, and sincere in speech or expression; Candidness: Freedom from bias; Fairness; Impartiality:

Carnage: The slaughter of a great number of people, as in battle; Butchery; Massacre.

Carnal: Pertaining to or characterized by the flesh or the body, its passions and appetites; Not spiritual; Merely human; Temporal; Worldly:

Carve – Carving: To cut (a solid material) so as to form something: To form from a solid material by cutting: You cut into slices or pieces, to carve figures, designs, etc.

Cognizant: Aware; Having knowledge. Having legal cognizance or jurisdiction.

Compassion: A feeling of deep sympathy and sorrow for another who is stricken by misfortune, accompanied by a strong desire to alleviate the suffering.

Compathy: Feelings, as happiness or grief, shared with another or others.

Concoct: To make by combining different ingredients; To invent; Make up; Contrive.

GOD KNOWS YOUR NAME!

Consecrated: To make or declare sacred or holy; Sanctify. To dedicate life to a specific purpose.

Correlation: Mutual relation of 2 or more things, parts, etc.:

Cumulative: Increasing or growing by accumulation or successive addition: combined parts or elements

Debauchery: Excessive indulgence unsensual pleasures; Intemperance.

Decimated: To destroy a great number or proportion of: To destroy or kill a large proportion of:

Denigrating: To treat or represent as lacking in value or importance; Belittle; Disparage:

Deplorable: Causing or being a subject for grief or regret; Lamentable: Causing or being a subject for censure, reproach, or disapproval; Wretched;

Depravity: The state or an instance of moral corruption

Deposition: A statement under oath, taken down in writing, to be used in court in place of the spoken testimony of the witness.

Dereliction: Deliberate or conscious neglect; Negligence; Delinquency: The act of abandoning something. The state of being abandoned.

Despair: Loss of hope; Hopelessness. To lose, give up, or be without hope.

Disdain: To look upon or treat with contempt; Despise; Scorn.

Dispensation: The divine ordering of the affairs of the world. A certain order, system, or arrangement; Administration or management.

Effervescent: Effervescing; Bubbling. Vivacious; Merry; Lively; Sparkling. High-spirited; Fizzy, Animated, Ebullient, Enthusiastic, Lighthearted.

Embark: To venture or invest (something). To start an enterprise, business, etc.

Empathy: The psychological identification with or vicarious experiencing of the feelings, thoughts, or attitudes of another.

Enamoured: In love; Captivated; Charmed

Enunciate: To utter or pronounce (words, sentences

etc.), in an articulate or a particular manner.

Escapades: Reckless adventures or wild pranks.

Exonerated: To clear, as of an accusation; Free from guilt or blame; Exculpate

Explicit: Fully and clearly expressed or demonstrated; Leaving nothing merely implied; Unequivocal: An explicit act of violence; Clearly developed or formulated: Definite and unreserved in expression; Outspoken:

GOD KNOWS YOUR NAME!

Exposé: A public exposure or revelation, as of something discreditable:

Extinction: Suppression; Abolition; Annihilation: A coming to an end or dying out: The reduction or loss of a conditioned response as a result of the absence or withdrawal of reinforcement.

Façade: A front or outer appearance, especially a deceptive one.

Fathom: To penetrate to the truth of; Comprehend; Understand:

Fleeting: Passing swiftly; Vanishing quickly;

Fruition: Attainment of anything desired; Realization; Accomplishment: Consummation, accomplishment, fulfillment, achievement, completion, perfection, result. Enjoyment, as of something attained or realized.

Garnered: To get; Acquire; Earn:

Girded: To surround; Enclose; Hem in. To prepare (oneself) for action: To provide, equip, or invest, as with power or strength.

Grotesque: [groh-tesk] Odd or unnatural in shape, appearance, or character; Fantastically ugly or absurd; Bizarre.

Hooch: A thatched hut of southeast Asia. Any living quarters, as a barracks. A prostitute's dwelling.

Immature: Not mature, ripe, developed, perfected, etc. Emotionally undeveloped; Juvenile; childish. Youthful ; Premature.

Implicit: Implied, rather than expressly stated: Unquestioning or unreserved; Unconditional: Potentially contained (usually followed by in):

In: Located or situated within; Inner; Internal:

Indicative: Showing, signifying, or pointing out; Expressive or suggestive.

Indulgence: Gratification of desire. A catering to someone's mood or whim.

Ingratiating: Charming; Agreeable; Pleasing.

Inkling: A slight suggestion or indication; Hint; A vague idea or notion; Slight understanding:

Inquest: A legal or judicial inquiry, usually before a jury, especially an investigation made by a coroner into the cause of a death.

Insatiable: Not able to be satisfied or satiated; Greedy or unappeasable

Insignificant: Unimportant, trifling, or petty: Too small to be important: Of no consequence, influence, or distinction: Without weight of character; Contemptible: Without meaning; Meaningless: A word, thing, or person without significance.

Jargon: Unintelligible or meaningless talk or writing; Gibberish. Any talk or writing that one does not understand.

Jehovah: A name of God in the Old Testament; A rendering of the ineffable name; JHVH, in the Hebrew Scriptures. (in modern Christian use) God.

Mantle: A garment regarded as a symbol of someone's power or authority: Anything that covers completely or envelops:

Mar: To damage or spoil to a certain extent; Render less perfect, attractive, useful, etc.; Impair or spoil: To disfigure, deface, or scar:

Martyrs: A person who willingly suffers death rather than renounce his or her religion. A person who is put to death or endures great suffering on behalf of any belief, principle, or cause: A person who undergoes severe or constant suffering: To torment or torture.

Masquerade: False outward show; Façade; Pretense: Activity, existence, etc., under false pretenses: To go about under false pretenses or a false character; Assume the character of; Give oneself out to be: To disguise oneself.

GOD KNOWS YOUR NAME!

Menace: Something that threatens to cause evil, harm, injury, etc.; A threat: A person whose actions, attitudes, or ideas are considered dangerous or harmful: An extremely annoying person.

Menagerie: An unusual & varied group of people. A collection of wild or unusual animals, especially for exhibition. A place where they are kept or exhibited.

Moniker: A person's name, especially a nickname or alias.

Monogamous: The state or practice of having only one husband or wife over a period of time. The practice of having only one mate.

Naïve: Having or showing a lack of experience, judgment, or information;

Novice: A recent convert to Christianity. A person new to the circumstances, work, etc., in which he or she is placed; Beginner; A person newly become a church member.

Of: Used to indicate possession, origin, or association:

Ominous: Portending evil or harm; Foreboding evil; Threatening; Inauspicious: Indicating the nature of a future event, for good or evil;

GOD KNOWS YOUR NAME!

Omniscient: The Omniscient, GOD. Having complete or unlimited knowledge, awareness, or understanding; Perceiving all things.

Palpable: Readily or plainly seen, heard, perceived, etc.; Obvious; Evident: Capable of being touched or felt; Tangible.

Philanderer: Sex with women one cannot or will not marry;

Pilfering: To steal, especially in small quantities.

Pillage: To strip ruthlessly of money or goods by open violence, as in war; Plunder:

Pinnacle: The highest or culminating point, as of success, power, fame, etc.

Pivotal: Of vital or critical importance:

Pragmatic: Of or relating to a practical point of view or practical considerations. Involving everyday or practical business. Of or concerned with the affairs of a state or community.

Plight: A condition, state, or situation, especially an unfavorable or unfortunate one:

Precluded: To prevent the presence, existence, or occurrence of; Make impossible: To exclude or debar from something.

Prevails: To prove superior; Gain mastery. To be or appear as the most important feature;

Prevalent: Widespread; Of wide extent or occurrence; In general use or acceptance. Having the superiority or ascendancy.

Privy: Participating in the knowledge of something private or secret.

Prodigal: A person who is wasteful of his or her money, possessions, etc.; Spendthrift: Wastefully or recklessly extravagant: Giving or yielding profusely; Very generous; Lavish; Lavishly abundant; Profuse:

Promiscuous: Characterized by or involving indiscriminate mingling or association, especially having sexual relations with a number of partners on a casual basis.

Propensity: A natural inclination or tendency:

Prowess: Exceptional or superior ability, skill, or strength: Exceptional valor, bravery, or ability, especially in combat or battle.

Quickening: To cause life. To revive; Restore life to:

Recesses: A receding part or space. A secluded or secret place; Recesses of the spirit and mind.

Recourse: Access or resort to a person or thing for help or protection:

Regalia: Rich, fancy, or dressy clothing; Finery.

Reprobated: A depraved, unprincipled, or wicked person: A person rejected by God and beyond hope of salvation.

Reverberate: To cast back or reflect; To reecho or resound: To be reflected many times, as sound waves from the walls of a confined space.

Rhetoric: The art or science of all specialized literary uses of language in prose or verse, including the figures of speech. The ability to use language effectively. The art of making persuasive speeches; Oratory. The undue use of exaggeration or display;

Scapegoat: A person or group made to bear the blame for others or to suffer in their place. A goat let loose in the wilderness on Yom Kippur after the high priest symbolically laid the sins of the people on its head.

Sensitivity: The state or quality of being sensitive; Sensitiveness. The ability of an organism or part of an organism to react to stimuli; Irritability. Degree of susceptibility to stimulation.

Shunned: To keep away from (a place, person, object, etc.), from motives of dislike, caution, etc.; Take pains to avoid.

Squelched: To strike or press with crushing force; Crush down; Squash.

Striation: The marks or stripes: Scratches and scars from stress and life.

Subservient: Serving or acting in a subordinate capacity; Excessively submissive; Useful in promoting a purpose or end.

Substantive: Real or actual. Of considerable amount or quantity. Having practical importance, value, or effect:

Succumb: To give way to superior force; Yield: To yield to disease, wounds, old age, etc.; Die.

Sympathy: The fact or power of sharing the feelings of another, especially in sorrow or trouble; Fellow feeling, compassion, or commiseration.

Tarmac: A road, airport runway, parking area, etc., paved with a layer of tar.

Transcends: To rise above or go beyond; Overpass; Exceed: To outdo or exceed in excellence, elevation, extent, degree, etc.; Surpass; Excel.

Transgression: A breach of a law, etc; Sin or crime.

Trepidation: Tremulous fear, alarm, or agitation; Perturbation. Trembling or quivering movement; Tremor. A state of anxious fear; Apprehension.

Tyro: A beginner in learning anything; novice.

Unanimity: A consensus or undivided opinion:

GOD KNOWS YOUR NAME!

Vernacular: The language or vocabulary peculiar to a class or profession. The native speech or language of a place.

Visceral: Characterized by or proceeding from intuition or instinct rather than intellect:

Wane: to decrease in strength, intensity, etc.:
To decline in power, importance, prosperity, etc.:
To draw to a close; approach an end:

Wax: To increase in extent, quantity, intensity, power, etc.: To grow or become:

Whoremonger: A person who consorts with whores.

www.ingramcontent.com/pod-product-compliance
Lightning Source LLC
Chambersburg PA
CBHW030544080526
44585CB00012B/247